150 PERFECT ITALIAN RECIPES

150 PERFECT
ITALIAN RECIPES

Marina Filippelli

An Hachette UK Company
www.hachette.co.uk

First published in Great Britain in 2009 by Hamlyn,
a division of Octopus Publishing Group Ltd
Endeavour House, 189 Shaftesbury Avenue, WC2H 8JY
www.octopusbooks.co.uk

This exclusive edition published in 2011

ISBN: 978-0-600-62430-1

A CIP catalogue record for this book is available from
the British Library

Printed and bound in China

1 2 3 4 5 6 7 8 9 10

Both metric and imperial measurements have
been given in all recipes. Use one set of measurements
only, and not a mixture of both.

Standard level spoon measurements are used in all recipes.
1 tablespoon = one 15 ml spoon
1 teaspoon = one 5 ml spoon

Ovens should be preheated to the specified temperature –
if using a fan-assisted oven, follow the manufacturer's
instructions for adjusting the time and the temperature.

Fresh herbs should be used unless otherwise stated.

Medium eggs should be used unless otherwise stated.

The Department of Health advises that eggs should not be
consumed raw. This book contains some dishes made with
raw or lightly cooked eggs. It is prudent for vulnerable people
such as pregnant and nursing mothers, invalids, the elderly,
babies and young children to avoid uncooked or lightly
cooked dishes made with eggs. Once prepared, these dishes
should be kept refrigerated and used promptly.

This book includes dishes made with nuts and nut derivatives.
It is advisable for those with known allergic reactions to nuts
and nut derivatives and those who may be potentially
vulnerable to these allergies, such as pregnant and nursing
mothers, invalids, the elderly, babies and children, to avoid
dishes made with nuts and nut oils. It is also prudent to check
the labels of pre-prepared ingredients for the possible
inclusion of nut derivatives.

contents

introduction   6

antipasti & salads   8

pasta & pizza   34

soups, rice & polenta   58

fish & seafood   84

meat & poultry   98

vegetables & legumes   120

desserts   134

index   158

acknowledgements   160

introduction

Italian food is now so popular that classics such as lasagne or tiramisu have become household favourites in all corners of the world. Fuss-free homely food, fresh ingredients and simple techniques all make for a cuisine that has instant appeal to the modern cook.

the Italian larder

The Italian cook depends on a well-stocked larder. Most of these ingredients are available in supermarkets, with only the more unusual ones requiring a trip to an Italian deli.

anchovies can be bought fresh or preserved in salt or oil. We used the preserved fish.

capers Small flower buds preserved in salt or brine. Rinse in cold water before using.

cheeses *Mozzarella* can be made from cows' milk or water buffaloes' milk. Cows' milk mozzarella is adequate for cooking, but if you are planning to eat your mozzarella fresh, it's worth splashing out on buffalo mozzarella. Only buy mozzarella kept in water.

Parmesan Parmigiano Reggiano is used extensively in Italian cooking. *Grana Padano* is similar to Parmesan and is a more economical choice for cooking.

Pecorino There are different varieties of this sheep's milk cheese, which can be aged until ready for the table or matured until dry and crumbly, to be used grated in cooking.

Ricotta A naturally low-fat soft cheese usually made from cows' milk.

Fontina A mild cheese which melts evenly and smoothly, making it perfect for cooking.

Gorgonzola and *dolcelatte* Both these blue cheeses are often used in pasta sauces. Gorgonzola is the stronger, while dolcelatte is creamy, with a milder, more delicate flavour.

Mascarpone A full-fat, thick cream cheese with a rich, smooth texture and mild flavour.

hams *Prosciutto crudo* ('raw ham') is the most commonly known Italian ham, of which the most famous variety is Parma ham. *Prosciutto cotto* is cooked ham.

olive oil For best results, it is essential to use extra virgin in recipes where the oil is not cooked or where it features as one of the main ingredients. Less expensive olive oil can be used for frying or sautéing vegetables at the beginning of cooking.

pasta can be made with or without egg, using durum wheat and/or soft wheat flour Buy the best you can afford and choose authentic Italian brands.

polenta This coarsely ground corn flour is cooked in water to the consistency of mashed potatoes. Once cold, soft polenta sets into a rigid block that can be topped with other ingredients and grilled. We used instant polenta for the recipes in this book.

pulses Beans and chickpeas are eaten fresh when in season, but when cooking them from dry, they need soaking overnight in cold water. Canned pulses, rinsed, can be used if time is short. You will need twice the quantity of canned beans to dried.

risotto rice Avoid generically labelled risotto rice and opt instead for one of three specific varieties grown in the Po Valley: arborio, carnaroli and vialone nano.

techniques

cleaning mussels Scrub mussels under cold running water. Pull away the 'beards' and discard any open shells that are broken or any that remain open when tapped. Soak in plenty of cold water for 30 minutes, then drain and rinse again in cold running water. Put in a bowl, cover with a wet tea towel and keep refrigerated until needed.

cleaning clams Wash the clams under cold running water, discarding any that are broken or that remain open when tapped. Soak in plenty of cold water for 30 minutes, then drain and rinse again in cold running water. Place in a bowl, cover with a wet tea towel and keep refrigerated until needed.

cleaning squid Wash the squid under cold running water. Pull the tentacles away from the body. The squid's entrails will come out easily. Remove the clear piece of cartilage inside the body cavity and discard. Wash the body thoroughly, pulling away the pinkish membrane. Cut between the tentacles and head, discarding the head and entrails.

basic pizza dough

Makes **4**
Preparation time **15 minutes**, plus rising

7 g (¼ oz) **fresh yeast** or 1 teaspoon **fast-action dried yeast**
pinch of **caster sugar**
500 g (1 lb) **plain flour**, plus extra for dusting
350 ml (12 fl oz) **lukewarm water**
1 ½ teaspoons **salt**

Dissolve the yeast in a bowl with the sugar, 2 tablespoons of the flour and 50 ml (2 fl oz) of the measured water. Leave to stand for 5 minutes until the mixture starts to form bubbles, then add the remaining water. Add the salt and half the remaining flour and stir with one hand until you have a paste-like mixture. Gradually add the remaining flour, working the mixture until you have a moist dough. Shape into a ball, cover with a moist cloth and leave to rest in a warm place for 5 minutes. Lightly dust a work surface with flour and knead the dough for 10 minutes until smooth and elastic. Shape into 4 equal-sized balls and place, spaced apart, on a lightly oiled tray. Cover with a moist cloth and leave to rise in a warm place for 1 hour. Use according to the recipe.

fried vegetables in batter

Serves **6**
Preparation time **15 minutes**
Cooking time **15 minutes**

100 g (3½ oz) **cauliflower**
100 g (3½ oz) **broccoli**
1 **red pepper**
1 **courgette**
1 **onion**
75 g (3 oz) **plain flour**, for
   dusting
sunflower oil, for deep-frying
6 **flat leaf parsley sprigs**
salt and **pepper**

Batter
2 **eggs**, lightly beaten
1 tablespoon **olive oil**
300 ml (½ pint) **chilled lager**
pinch of **salt**
225 g (7½ oz) **plain flour**,
   sifted

Combine all the ingredients for the batter in a large bowl, mixing well but not worrying about any lumps that may have formed. Cover and chill while you prepare the vegetables.

Cut the cauliflower and broccoli into small florets. Core and deseed the pepper, then cut it lengthways into 8 strips. Slice the courgette into 1 cm (½ inch) rounds and cut the onion into 8 wedges. Tip the flour into a bowl and season with salt and pepper, then toss in the prepared vegetables.

Heat enough oil for deep-frying in a deep saucepan to 180–190°C (350–375°F), or until a cube of bread browns in 30 seconds. Take 5 or 6 vegetable pieces from the flour, shake off any excess, then plunge into the batter. Lift out, letting the batter drip off slightly, then carefully plunge into the hot oil. Cook for about 3 minutes until golden. Remove with a slotted spoon and drain on kitchen paper. Once all the vegetables are cooked, lightly dust the parsley sprigs with flour, dip in the batter and cook for 1–2 minutes, or until just golden.

Season the vegetables and parsley with salt and serve immediately.

For basil & lemon batter, make the batter as above, but add the grated rind of 1 lemon and 3 tablespoons chopped basil. Cover and leave to infuse in the refrigerator for at least 30 minutes before using as above. The parsley sprigs can be replaced with 8 drained anchovy fillets in olive oil.

rocket & garlic crumbed mussels

Serves **4**
Preparation time **15 minutes**
Cooking time **10 minutes**

25 g (1 oz) **wild rocket leaves**
1 **garlic clove**
50 g (2 oz) **fresh white breadcrumbs**
4 tablespoons **extra virgin olive oil**
1 kg (2 lb) **mussels**, cleaned (see page 7)
salt and **pepper**
lemon wedges, to serve

Process the rocket and garlic in a food processor until roughly chopped. Add the breadcrumbs and pulse until combined, then stir in the oil. Season with salt and pepper. Cover and chill until needed.

Put the mussels in a large saucepan with a tight-fitting lid and add water to a depth of 2.5 cm (1 inch). Cover and bring to the boil over a high heat. Cook the mussels, shaking the pan frequently, for 2–3 minutes, or until the shells have opened. Drain, discarding any that remain closed. Pull away and discard the empty shell halves, reserving only the halves with the mussels attached.

Place the mussels, flesh-side up, on a baking sheet. Divide the breadcrumb topping between the mussels and cook on the top shelf of a preheated high grill for 1–2 minutes until the breadcrumbs are golden. Serve immediately with lemon wedges on the side.

For tomato & parsley crumbed scallops, make the breadcrumb mixture as above, but replace the rocket with 20 g (¾ oz) flat leaf parsley and 4 drained sun-dried tomatoes in oil. Instead of the mussels, use 12 opened scallops. Loosen the scallops from their base shell by cutting through the muscle that attaches them to the shell with a small, sharp knife. Divide the breadcrumb topping between the scallops and cook under the grill as above, but increase the cooking time to 2–3 minutes.

broad bean bruschetta

Serves **4**
Preparation time **15 minutes**
Cooking time **3 minutes**

5 tablespoons **extra virgin
  olive oil**, plus extra for
  drizzling
2 **garlic cloves**, 1 crushed and
  1 left whole
pinch of **crushed dried
  chillies**
handful of **mint leaves**
250 g (8 oz) shelled **broad
  beans**, thawed if frozen,
  skins removed
40 g (1½ oz) **Pecorino
  cheese**, grated
1 small **ciabatta loaf**, cut into
  8 thin slices
salt and **pepper**
Parmesan cheese shavings,
  to serve

Combine the oil, crushed garlic, crushed chillies and mint in a bowl and leave to infuse for 10 minutes.

Meanwhile, lightly crush the broad beans in a separate bowl with a fork. Season with salt and pepper, then toss into the oil mixture with the Pecorino. Toast the bread slices on both sides under a preheated medium grill or in a preheated ridged griddle pan or over a barbecue.

Rub the toasted slices with the remaining garlic. Top with the broad bean mixture and drizzle over a little oil. Scatter with Parmesan shavings and serve immediately.

For Parmesan & cannellini bean bruschetta,

combine 2 crushed garlic cloves, 1 teaspoon chopped rosemary and 4 tablespoons extra virgin olive oil in a bowl and leave to infuse for 10 minutes. Drain a 400 g (13 oz) can cannellini beans, rinse, then drain again. Lightly crush with a fork and stir into the oil mixture with 2 tablespoons freshly grated Parmesan cheese, salt to taste and a large pinch of crushed dried chillies. Serve on toasted bread slices, as above, drizzled with a little extra oil and scattered with Parmesan shavings.

carpaccio of fresh tuna

Serves **4**

Preparation time **10 minutes**, plus freezing

250 g (8 oz) piece of **tuna loin**
juice of **3 lemons**
150 ml (¼ pint) **extra virgin olive oil**
1 **garlic clove**, finely chopped
1 tablespoon **salted capers**, rinsed
125 g (4 oz) **wild rocket leaves**
salt and **pepper**
Parmesan cheese shavings, to serve

Trim the tuna of any membrane or gristle. Wrap tightly in clingfilm and put in the freezer for about 1 hour until just frozen but not rock solid.

Meanwhile, whisk together the lemon juice, oil, garlic and capers in a bowl. Add salt and pepper to taste and whisk until emulsified.

Unwrap the tuna and thinly slice with a sharp, thin-bladed knife. Arrange the slices on 4 large serving plates. Spoon the dressing over the tuna. Top with a tangle of rocket leaves and scatter with Parmesan shavings.

For fresh swordfish carpaccio, replace the tuna with 250 g (8 oz) piece of swordfish. Freeze, thinly slice and arrange on plates as above. Whisk together the lemon juice, olive oil and garlic, also adding 2 tablespoons chopped flat leaf parsley, instead of the capers. Spoon over the plated fish and top with the rocket. Omit the Parmesan cheese.

balsamic figs with parma ham

Serves **4**
Preparation time **5 minutes**
Cooking time **4–5 minutes**

8 **ripe fresh figs**
2 tablespoons **balsamic
vinegar**
extra virgin olive oil, for
drizzling
12 slices of **Parma ham**
50 g (2 oz) **wild rocket leaves**
salt and **pepper**

Cut the figs in half and arrange, cut-side up, on a baking sheet. Brush with the vinegar and lightly drizzle with oil. Season with a little salt and a generous grinding of pepper.

Cook under a preheated high grill for 4–5 minutes until heated through and a little charred.

Arrange 3 slices of Parma ham on each serving plate. Top with the grilled figs and scatter with rocket leaves. Drizzle over a little more oil and serve while the figs are still warm.

For minted melon with Parma ham, put a sliced small, ripe melon on a platter with 12 slices of Parma ham, then give this simple, classic Italian *antipasto* a modern twist by scattering it with 5 torn mint leaves and drizzling over a little extra virgin olive oil.

salt cod pâté

Serves **4**
Preparation time **10 minutes**,
   plus soaking
Cooking time **15 minutes**

400 g (13 oz) **salt cod**
1 **bay leaf**
3 **garlic cloves**, peeled but
   kept whole
pinch of **crushed dried
   chillies**
milk, for poaching
75 ml (3 fl oz) **extra virgin
   olive oil**, plus extra for
   drizzling
2 tablespoons roughly
   chopped **flat leaf parsley**
1 **red chilli**, deseeded and
   finely chopped
salt (optional)
1 small **ciabatta loaf**, cut into
   8 slices and griddled or
   toasted, to serve

Soak the salt cod in a large bowl of cold water for 48 hours, changing the water 5–6 times a day.

Drain the cod and put in a saucepan with the bay leaf, garlic and crushed chillies. Pour in enough milk to completely submerge the cod. Bring to the boil, then reduce the heat and simmer for 10 minutes. Remove the cod with a slotted spoon, reserving the poaching milk and garlic cloves, and leave until cool enough to handle. Break into flakes, removing and discarding the skin and any bones.

Process the cod with 5 tablespoons of the reserved poaching milk and the garlic cloves in a food processor until smooth. With the motor running, add the oil in a very slow, steady stream until incorporated.

Stir in the parsley, chopped fresh chilli and, if necessary, a little salt. Drizzle with oil and serve with the griddled or toasted bread.

For salt cod in batter, prepare the batter as directed on page 8. Soak and cook 500 g (1 lb) salt cod as above, then drain thoroughly and cut into 5 cm (2 inch) pieces. Heat enough sunflower oil for deep-frying in a deep saucepan to 180–190°C (350–375°F), or until a cube of bread browns in 30 seconds. Pat the salt cod pieces dry with kitchen paper, then dip in seasoned plain flour, followed by the batter. Add to the hot oil, in batches, and cook for 5–6 minutes until golden. Drain on kitchen paper. Serve with lemon wedges.

mozzarella in carrozza

Serves **4**
Preparation time **10 minutes**
Cooking time **15 minutes**

3 **eggs**, lightly beaten
3 tablespoons **full-fat milk**
50 g (2 oz) **plain flour**
200 g (7 oz) **mozzarella cheese** (drained weight), cut into 5 mm (¼ inch) thick slices
8 slices of **white bread**
12 **basil leaves**
4 tablespoons **olive oil**
salt and **pepper**

Combine the eggs and milk in a bowl and season lightly with salt and pepper. Put the flour in a separate bowl.

Divide the mozzarella slices between 4 bread slices and top each with 3 basil leaves. Lay a second bread slice on top of each to make 4 sandwiches. Press down firmly on each sandwich with the heel of your hand, then cut off and discard the crusts.

Heat half the oil in a large frying pan over a medium heat. Turn 2 of the sandwiches, 1 at a time, briefly in the flour to give a light coating, then dip in the egg mixture, making sure that they are well covered. Add to the pan and cook for 3–4 minutes on each side until golden and crisp. Remove and keep warm in a low oven while you cook the second batch of sandwiches in the remaining oil. Serve with a few lettuce leaves, if liked.

For spiced Parma ham & mozzarella in carrozza, combine the eggs and milk as above, but season with salt and ¼ teaspoon chilli powder. Follow the recipe to fill the sandwiches with the mozzarella slices together with 1 slice of Parma ham for each, omitting the basil, then coat and cook as above.

prosciutto-wrapped grissini

Makes **20–25**
Preparation time **15 minutes**
Cooking time **5–8 minutes**

½ quantity **Basic Pizza Dough**
(see page 7)
plain flour, for dusting
slices of **prosciutto**, cut into
strips, to serve

Flavourings
coarse sea salt
sesame seeds
poppy seeds
cracked black pepper

Combine the dough balls and roll the dough out thinly on a well-floured work surface into a rectangle. Following the long side of the rectangle, cut into 5 mm (¼ inch) strips. Lightly roll each strip and taper the ends.

Brush the grissini lightly with water and sprinkle with the flavouring of your choice. Transfer to a baking sheet and bake in a preheated oven, 200°C (400°F), Gas Mark 6, for 5–8 minutes until crisp and brown. Leave to cool completely.

Twist strips of prosciutto around the grissini to serve.

For cheesy prosciutto-wrapped asparagus, cut
6 slices prosciutto in half, to give you 12 long strips. Wrap these around 12 asparagus spears and lay them on a baking sheet. Drizzle with 1 tablespoon olive oil and scatter 1 tablespoon grated Parmesan over the asparagus. Cook under a preheated grill on high, for 5–6 minutes, until the asparagus is just tender and the ham crispy.

griddled vegetable platter

Serves **4**
Preparation time **10 minutes**,
   plus marinating
Cooking time **20 minutes**

2 **courgettes**, sliced
   lengthways into 5 mm
   (¼ inch) thick slices
1 **aubergine**, sliced
   lengthways into 5 mm
   (¼ inch) thick slices
1 **yellow pepper**, cored,
   deseeded and cut into
   2.5 cm (1 inch) wide slices
1 **red pepper**, cored,
   deseeded and cut into
   2.5 cm (1 inch) wide slices
100 ml (3½ fl oz) **extra virgin
   olive oil**
2 **garlic cloves**, crushed
large pinch of **crushed dried
   chillies**
handful of small **mint** and/or
   basil leaves
salt

Toss all the prepared vegetables in 2 tablespoons of
the oil until well coated.

Heat a ridged griddle pan over a high heat until
smoking hot. Add the courgettes and aubergine in
batches and cook for 2–3 minutes on each side.
Transfer to a bowl and toss with the remaining oil, the
garlic and crushed chillies. Set aside.

Add the peppers in batches to the reheated griddle pan
and cook for 3–4 minutes on each side, then combine
with the courgettes and aubergine. Season with salt
and toss in the herbs.

Cover and leave to marinate at room temperature for
30 minutes. Serve with slices of country bread.

**For griddled courgettes with lemon, mint &
Parmesan**, omit the peppers and slice 4 large
courgettes lengthways into 5 mm (¼ inch) slices, toss
with oil and then griddle as above. Transfer to a bowl
and toss with the remaining oil, the garlic and crushed
chillies as above, adding a handful of small mint leaves,
torn, but not the basil. Leave to marinate as above,
then serve with a generous topping of Parmesan
cheese shavings and the finely grated rind of ½ lemon.

tuna & borlotti bean salad

Serves **4**

Preparation time **15 minutes**, plus marinating

Cooking time **3 minutes**

400 g (13 oz) can **borlotti beans**, drained and rinsed
1 tablespoon **water** (optional)
2 tablespoons **extra virgin olive oil**
2 **garlic cloves**, crushed
1 **red chilli**, deseeded and finely chopped
2 **celery sticks**, thinly sliced
½ **red onion**, cut into thin wedges
200 g (7 oz) can **tuna in olive oil**, drained and flaked
finely grated **rind** and **juice** of 1 **lemon**
50 g (2 oz) **wild rocket leaves**
salt and **pepper**

Heat the borlotti beans in a saucepan over a medium heat for 3 minutes, adding the measurement water if starting to stick to the base.

Put the oil, garlic and chilli in a large bowl. Stir in the celery, onion and hot beans and season with salt and pepper. Cover and leave to marinate at room temperature for at least 30 minutes and up to 4 hours.

Stir in the tuna and lemon rind and juice. Gently toss in the rocket leaves, taste and adjust the seasoning with extra salt, pepper and lemon juice, if necessary.

For a mixed bean salad, heat the borlotti beans as above with a 400 g (13 oz) can drained and rinsed cannellini beans. Leave to marinate with the other salad ingredients as above, but also adding 2 tablespoons roughly chopped flat leaf parsley. After marinating, toss in 50 g (2 oz) lambs' lettuce, season with salt and pepper and serve.

stuffed peppers

Serves **6**

Preparation time **25 minutes**,
   plus steaming and marinating

Cooking time **15 minutes**

6 **red**, **orange** or **yellow**
   peppers
12 **artichoke hearts in olive**
   oil, drained
24 **anchovy fillets in olive oil**,
   drained
2 **garlic cloves**, sliced
1 tablespoon chopped
   oregano
extra virgin olive oil, for
   drizzling
2 **hard-boiled eggs**, finely
   chopped
salt and **pepper**

Put the whole peppers in a grill pan and cook under a preheated high grill or over a barbecue until the skins begin to char. Turn the peppers and continue to cook until charred all over.

Transfer the peppers to a plastic bag, seal and leave to steam for 10 minutes. Peel off the skins, then cut the peppers in half lengthways through the stalks and remove and discard the cores and seeds. Arrange the peppers, cut-side up, in a shallow dish.

Cut the artichokes in half and put 2 halves in each pepper half. Lay 2 anchovy fillets over the artichokes. Season well with salt and pepper. Scatter over the garlic and oregano, then drizzle with oil.

Cover and leave to marinate in the refrigerator overnight. Serve at room temperature, sprinkled with the chopped hard-boiled eggs.

For grilled peppers in herb oil, grill and peel the peppers as above. Core and deseed then cut the flesh into 2.5 cm (1 inch) strips. Roughly chop 2 rosemary sprigs and 2 thyme sprigs. Toss them into a bowl with the peppers, also adding 1 sliced garlic clove and 1 whole dried chilli. Season with salt and pour in 50 ml (2 fl oz) extra virgin olive oil. Cover and marinate in the refrigerator overnight.

seafood salad

Serves **4**

Preparation time **20 minutes**, plus chilling

Cooking time **10 minutes**

500 g (1 lb) **mussels**, cleaned (see page 7)

300 g (10 oz) **clams**, cleaned (see page 7)

1 **onion**, quartered

1 **bay leaf**

300 g (10 oz) **small squid**, cleaned (see page 7) and cut into 2.5 cm (1 inch) rounds

300 g (10 oz) **raw peeled king prawns**

8 small **shelled scallops**, with or without roe

juice of 2 **lemons**

2 **garlic cloves**, finely chopped

4 tablespoons **olive oil**

2 **celery sticks**, thinly sliced

1 **carrot**, cut into small cubes

1 **red pepper**, cored, deseeded and cut into small cubes

3 **spring onions**, thinly sliced

salt and **pepper**

crusty bread, to serve

Put the shellfish and 100 ml (3½ fl oz) water in a large saucepan with a tight-fitting lid. Cover and bring to the boil over a high heat. Cook, shaking the pan frequently, for 4–5 minutes, or until the shells have opened. Remove with a slotted spoon, discarding any that remain closed. Remove the flesh from the shells and put in a large bowl.

Return the pan with the cooking liquid to a high heat, add 400 ml (14 fl oz) water, the onion and bay leaf and bring to the boil. Add the seafood and cook for 2–3 minutes until the prawns turn pink and the scallops are opaque all the way though. Remove with a slotted spoon and add to the shellfish.

Boil the liquid until reduced to 50 ml (2 fl oz). Remove from the heat and stir in the lemon juice, garlic and oil. Season with salt and pepper, pour over the seafood and shellfish and toss well.

Leave to cool to room temperature, then toss in the remaining ingredients. Cover and chill for at least 30 minutes and up to 24 hours. Serve the salad with crusty bread.

For seafood rice salad, cook the shellfish, then the seafood as above. Remove from the pan, discard the onion and bay leaf and stir in a large pinch of saffron threads. Boil rapidly until reduced to 100 ml (3½ fl oz). Toss in 200 g (7 oz) freshly cooked long-grain rice. Remove from the heat and stir well. Add the seafood and remaining ingredients as above, but omit the red pepper.

crudités & garlic anchovy dip

Serves **4–6**
Preparation time **10 minutes**
Cooking time **15 minutes**

50 ml (2 fl oz) **milk**
6 **garlic cloves**, peeled but
   kept whole
150 g (5 oz) **anchovy fillets in
   olive oil**, drained and roughly
   chopped
75 g (3 oz) **butter**
75 ml (3 fl oz) **extra virgin
   olive oil**

Crudités
8 **baby carrots**, peeled
250 g (8 oz) **cauliflower
   florets**
4 **celery sticks**, cut in half
½ **red cabbage**, cut into thin
   wedges
5 **baby fennel**, cut in half
   lengthways

Put the milk, garlic and anchovies in a small saucepan over a low heat and cook gently for 15 minutes, without letting the milk come to the boil, until the anchovies have melted into the pan and the garlic is soft.

Use the back of a fork to mash the garlic against the side of the pan. Add the butter and oil and stir until the butter has melted. Transfer to a small serving bowl.

Arrange the crudités in a large serving dish, leaving space for the bowl of sauce, and serve while the sauce is still warm for dipping.

For garlic & caper mayonnaise, to serve in place of the garlic anchovy dip, put 2 egg yolks and 1 crushed garlic clove in a food processor. With the motor running, add 250 ml (8 fl oz) olive oil in a very slow, steady stream until incorporated, then stir in 1½ tablespoons roughly chopped, rinsed capers in brine. Season with salt and pepper and serve with the crudités as above.

orecchiette with broccoli

Serves **4**

Preparation time **10 minutes**

Cooking time **15 minutes**

500 g (1 lb) **broccoli**, roughly chopped

400 g (13 oz) **dried orecchiette**

5 tablespoons **extra virgin olive oil**

2 **anchovy fillets in olive oil**, drained and roughly chopped

large pinch of **crushed dried chillies**

2 **garlic cloves**, sliced

4 tablespoons freshly grated **Parmesan cheese**, plus extra to serve

Bring a large saucepan of salted water to the boil and tip in the broccoli and pasta. Cook for about 14 minutes, or according to the pasta packet instructions, until the pasta is al dente and the broccoli is cooked and starting to fall apart.

Meanwhile, pour the oil into a large frying pan and add the anchovies, crushed chillies and garlic and heat over a very low heat for 5–6 minutes until the anchovies have melted into the oil.

Drain the pasta, reserving a ladleful of the cooking water, and toss the pasta and broccoli into the pan with the anchovy oil. Toss over a high heat for 30 seconds, then pour in the reserved cooking water and continue stirring over the heat for a further 30 seconds. Work the Parmesan into the pasta, then serve with an extra scattering of Parmesan.

For penne with creamy cauliflower, follow the recipe as above, but replace the broccoli with 500 g (1 lb) roughly chopped cauliflower and the orecchiette with 400 g (13 oz) dried penne. Instead of adding the reserved cooking water to the pan at the end of the recipe, stir in 250 g (8 oz) crème fraîche with the Parmesan.

wild mushroom lasagne

Serves **6**

Preparation time **20 minutes**, plus cooling

Cooking time **45 minutes**

100 g (3½ oz) **unsalted butter**, plus extra for greasing

4 tablespoons **plain flour**

1 litre (1¾ pints) **milk**

large pinch of freshly grated **nutmeg**

3 tablespoons roughly chopped **flat leaf parsley**

5 tablespoons freshly grated **Parmesan cheese**

1 tablespoon **olive oil**

625 g (1¼ lb) **mixed wild mushrooms**, trimmed and thickly sliced

1 **garlic clove**, crushed

100 ml (3½ fl oz) **dry white wine**

25 g (1 oz) **dried porcini mushrooms**, soaked in 100 ml (3½ fl oz) hot water for 10 minutes

300 g (10 oz) **fresh lasagne sheets**

truffle oil, for drizzling

salt and **pepper**

Melt half the butter in a saucepan over a low heat. Add the flour and cook, stirring with a wooden spoon, for 1–2 minutes until a pale biscuit colour. Remove from the heat and gradually stir in the milk until smooth. Return to a medium heat and cook, stirring constantly, until thick and velvety. Add the nutmeg and season with salt and pepper, then stir in the parsley and 2 tablespoons of the Parmesan. Remove from the heat and leave to cool to room temperature.

Melt the remaining butter with the oil in a large, heavy-based frying pan. Add the fresh mushrooms and cook over a high heat for 2 minutes. Stir in the garlic and cook for 1 minute. Season with salt and pepper. Pour in the wine and porcini and their soaking water. Cook, stirring, until the liquid has evaporated. Stir into the white sauce.

Grease an ovenproof dish, about 19 x 30 cm (8 x 12 inches). Cover the base with a layer of slightly overlapping lasagne sheets. Top with a quarter of the sauce, then continue layering, finishing with a layer of sauce. Scatter with the remaining Parmesan. Bake in a preheated oven, 200°C (400°F), Gas Mark 6, for 30 minutes. Drizzle lightly with truffle oil and serve with a green salad, if liked.

For mushroom, blue cheese & spinach lasagne,

follow the recipe above, but stir 75 g (3 oz) chopped gorgonzola and 100 g (3½ oz) baby spinach into the white sauce instead of the parsley in the first step, then omit the dried porcini.

spaghetti with clams & chilli

Serves **4**
Preparation time **10 minutes**
Cooking time **20 minutes**

5 tablespoons **extra virgin olive oil**
2 **garlic cloves**, thinly sliced
¼ teaspoon **crushed dried chillies**
400 g (13 oz) **dried spaghetti**
150 ml (¼ pint) **dry white wine**
1 kg (2 lb) **clams**, cleaned (see page 7)
2 tablespoons roughly chopped **flat leaf parsley**

Heat the oil in the largest frying pan you have or a wok over a low heat. Add the garlic and crushed chillies and leave to infuse for 6–8 minutes. If the garlic begins to colour, remove the pan from the heat and leave to infuse in the heat of the pan.

Cook the pasta in a large saucepan of salted boiling water for 8–10 minutes, or according to the packet instructions, until al dente, then drain.

Meanwhile, increase the heat under the frying pan and pour in the wine. Boil for 1 minute, then add the clams and cook, stirring, for 4–5 minutes until the shells have opened. Stir in the drained pasta and the parsley and toss over a high heat for 30 seconds. Serve immediately.

For spaghetti with clams, pancetta & tomatoes,

heat the oil in a large frying pan or wok as above. Add 75 g (3 oz) cubed pancetta and cook for 3–4 minutes until golden and crisp. Add the garlic and leave to infuse over a low heat for 10 minutes. Cook the pasta as above. Add the wine to the frying pan and boil for 1 minute as above, then add the clams with 100 g (3½ oz) halved cherry tomatoes and complete the recipe as above.

roasted tomato & pancetta pasta

Serves **4**

Preparation time **5 minutes**

Cooking time **about 1 hour**

500 g (1 lb) **cherry tomatoes**

3 tablespoons **olive oil**

400 g (13 oz) **dried rigatoni**
or **penne**

100 g (3½ oz) **pancetta**,
cubed

1 **garlic clove**, thinly sliced

2 **shallots**, thinly sliced

large pinch of **crushed dried
chillies**

aged balsamic vinegar, for
drizzling

salt

Put the whole tomatoes in a large roasting tin and drizzle with 2 tablespoons of the oil. Slow-roast in a preheated oven, 150°C (300°F), Gas Mark 2, for 1 hour, or until they look semi-dried.

Meanwhile, cook the pasta in a large saucepan of salted boiling water for about 10–12 minutes, or according to the packet instructions, until al dente.

While the pasta is cooking, heat the remaining oil in a large frying pan. Add the pancetta, garlic, shallots and crushed chillies and cook over a low heat for 10 minutes, or until the shallots are golden and the pancetta nice and crispy.

Toss the roasted tomatoes into the frying pan, reserving a few for garnishing. Drain the pasta, reserving a ladleful of the cooking water. Add the pasta to the sauce and toss over a high heat for a few seconds. Add the reserved cooking water and continue tossing for another 30 seconds. Serve immediately, garnished with the reserved roasted tomatoes and a drizzle of aged balsamic vinegar.

For roasted tomato, pancetta & spinach salad, slow-roast the tomatoes and cook the pancetta with the garlic, shallots and crushed chillies as above. Toss all these ingredients into 75 g (3 oz) baby spinach in a salad bowl. Whisk together 2 tablespoons extra virgin olive oil, 2 teaspoons aged balsamic vinegar and salt to taste in a small bowl, add to the salad and toss to coat. Shave over some Parmesan cheese to serve.

spaghetti with charred asparagus

Serves **4**
Preparation time **10 minutes**
Cooking time **15 minutes**

500 g (1 lb) **thin asparagus spears**, trimmed
3–4 tablespoons **extra virgin olive oil**
juice of 1 **lemon**
375 g (12 oz) **dried spaghetti**
2 **garlic cloves**, roughly chopped
¼–½ teaspoon **dried chilli flakes**
25 g (1 oz) **basil leaves**
25 g (1 oz) freshly grated **Parmesan cheese**, plus extra to serve (optional)
salt and **pepper**

Brush the asparagus spears with a little of the oil. Cook in a preheated ridged griddle pan or under a preheated high grill, turning once, until charred and tender. Toss with a little more of the oil, half the lemon juice and salt and pepper. Set aside.

Cook the pasta in a large saucepan of salted boiling water for 8–10 minutes, or according to the packet instructions, until al dente.

Just before the pasta is cooked, heat the remaining oil in a large frying pan or wok over a medium heat. Add the garlic with a little salt and cook, stirring, for 3–4 minutes until softened but not browned. Add the chilli flakes and asparagus and heat through.

Drain the pasta, reserving a ladleful of the cooking water, and add both to the frying pan with the basil, remaining lemon juice, the Parmesan and pepper to taste. Serve immediately, with extra Parmesan, if liked.

For pasta salad with mozzarella & asparagus, complete the first step of the recipe as above and toss into 400 g (13 oz) freshly cooked penne. Toss in the remaining ingredients and leave to marinate while the pasta and asparagus cool to room temperature. Roughly chop 200 g (7 oz) mozzarella and toss into the pasta, adding extra olive oil, if needed.

pizza fiorentina

Serves **4**

Preparation time **10 minutes**,
plus making the pizza dough

Cooking time **35 minutes**

1 tablespoon **olive oil**, plus
extra for drizzling and glazing

2 **garlic cloves**, crushed

500 g (1 lb) **baby spinach**

1 quantity **Basic Pizza Dough**
(see page 7)

plain flour, for dusting

200 ml (7 fl oz) **passata**

200 g (7 oz) **mozzarella
cheese** (drained weight),
chopped

20 **black olives**

4 **eggs**

salt and **pepper**

Heat the oil in a large frying pan with the garlic for
15 seconds, then add the spinach and cook over a
high heat for 1–2 minutes until just wilted. Season
lightly with salt and pepper.

Heat a baking sheet in a preheated oven, 240°C
(475°F), Gas Mark 9. Place 1 pizza dough ball on
the base only of a well-floured, 23 cm (9 inch) loose-
bottomed tart tin. Push down on the dough with your
fingertips, pressing it out to fill the base, leaving the
border slightly thicker. If you get any tears, forcefully
pinch the dough around the hole back together.

Spoon 3 tablespoons of the passata over the base
and scatter with a quarter of the mozzarella, spinach
and olives. Crack 1 egg on to the pizza, drizzle with oil
and season lightly with salt and pepper. Brush the
border with oil to glaze. Remove the baking sheet from
the oven, slide the tin on to it, then quickly return to the
oven. Bake for 7–8 minutes until crisp and risen. Serve
immediately. As the first pizza cooks, prepare the next
for the oven.

For spinach, anchovy & caper pizza, cook the
spinach and prepare the pizza base as above. Brush
with olive oil, then top with a quarter of the mozzarella
and spinach, as above, omitting the olives and egg.
Arrange 5 drained anchovy fillets in olive oil over the
pizza and scatter with 1 teaspoon rinsed capers in
brine. Drizzle with chilli oil and cook as above. Repeat
to make 3 more pizzas.

prosciutto & artichoke sfincione

Serves **4**

Preparation time **30 minutes**, plus rising

Cooking time **15–20 minutes**

15 g (½ oz) **fresh yeast** or ½ tablespoon **fast-action dried yeast**

pinch of **caster sugar**

250 ml (8 fl oz) **lukewarm water**

375 g (12 oz) **plain flour**, plus extra for dusting

2 tablespoons **olive oil**, plus extra for oiling and drizzling

½ teaspoon **salt**

3 tablespoons **sun-dried tomato purée**

1 **mozzarella cheese**, weighing about 150 g (5 oz) (drained weight), thinly sliced

4 ripe **plum tomatoes**, cut into long wedges

8 **artichoke hearts in olive oil**, drained and halved

4 large **garlic cloves**, sliced

6 slices **prosciutto**

3 tablespoons freshly grated **Parmesan cheese**

basil leaves, to garnish

Cream the fresh yeast with the sugar in a bowl, then whisk in the water. For dried yeast, dissolve the yeast in a bowl with the sugar, water and 2 tablespoons of the flour. Cover with a moist cloth and leave to stand in a warm place for 10 minutes until foamy.

Sift the flour into a large bowl and make a well in the centre. Add the yeast mixture, oil and salt to the well and mix with a round-bladed knife, then with your hands, until the dough comes together. Knead on a floured work surface for about 10 minutes until smooth and elastic. It should be quite soft, but if it is too soft to handle, add a little more flour. Put in an oiled bowl, cover with a moist cloth and leave to rise in a warm place for 1 hour, or until doubled in size.

Knock the dough back and roll out to a 30 cm (12 inch) circle, leaving the border slightly thicker. Slide on to a large floured baking sheet.

Spread the tomato purée over the pizza base. Arrange half the mozzarella on top. Scatter over the tomatoes, artichokes and garlic. Drape the prosciutto over the pizza. Scatter over the Parmesan and remaining mozzarella. Drizzle with oil and bake in a preheated oven, 240°C, (475°F), Gas Mark 9, for 15–20 minutes until golden. Serve garnished with basil leaves.

For tomato, onion and anchovy sfincione, prepare the dough as above. For the topping, cook 1 large sliced onion in 2 tablespoons olive oil. Add 300 ml (½ pint) passata, 1 crushed garlic clove and 8 chopped anchovy fillets. Scatter with 150 g (5 oz) chopped mozzarella and bake as above.

pizza with speck & dolcelatte

Serves **4**

Preparation time **15 minutes**,
plus making the pizza dough

Cooking time **35 minutes**

200 ml (7 fl oz) **passata**

5 large **basil leaves**, torn, plus
extra to garnish

1 **garlic clove**, crushed

1 tablespoon **extra virgin
olive oil**, plus extra for
glazing

1 quantity **Basic Pizza Dough**
(see page 7)

plain flour, for dusting

125 g (4 oz) **mozzarella
cheese** (drained weight),
torn into chunks

12 slices of **speck**

75 g (3 oz) **dolcelatte cheese**,
broken into pieces

salt

Combine the passata, basil, garlic and oil in a
bowl. Season with salt, cover and leave to infuse
for 15 minutes.

Heat a baking sheet in a preheated oven, 240°C
(475°F), Gas Mark 9. Place 1 pizza dough ball on
the base only of a well-floured, 23 cm (9 inch) loose-
bottomed tart tin. Push down on the dough with your
fingertips, pressing it out to fill the base, leaving the
border slightly thicker. If you get any tears, forcefully
pinch the dough around the hole back together.

Spoon 3 tablespoons of the passata mix over the base
and scatter with a quarter of the mozzarella. Brush the
border with oil to glaze. Remove the heated baking
sheet from the oven, slide the tin on to it, then quickly
return to the oven. Bake for 7–8 minutes until crisp and
risen. Top with 3 slices of speck, then half the dolcelatte.
Serve immediately, garnished with a little torn basil. As
the first pizza cooks, prepare the next for the oven.

For pizza with smoked mozzarella, Parma ham
& rocket, prepare the passata mixture and pizza base
as above. Top the tomato mixture with 125 g (4 oz)
smoked mozzarella slices, divided between the
4 pizza bases. Bake as above, then top each pizza
with 3 slices of Parma ham and 15 g (½ oz) wild
rocket leaves.

aubergine, basil & ricotta pizza

Serves **4**

Preparation time **10 minutes**, plus making the pizza dough

Cooking time **50 minutes**

150 ml (¼ pint) **passata**

5 large **basil leaves**, torn

1 **garlic clove**, crushed

2–3 small–medium **aubergines**, sliced lengthways into 5 mm (¼ inch) thick slices

1 quantity **Basic Pizza Dough** (see page 7)

plain flour, for dusting

125 g (4 oz) **ricotta cheese**, broken into small chunks

75 g (3 oz) **mozzarella cheese** (drained weight), roughly chopped

olive oil, for glazing

salt

basil leaves, to garnish

Combine the passata, basil and garlic in a bowl. Season lightly with salt, cover and leave to infuse while you cook the aubergines.

Heat a ridged griddle pan over a high heat until smoking hot. Add the aubergine, in batches, and cook for 2 minutes on each side until charred on the outside and soft all the way through.

Heat a baking sheet in a preheated oven, 240°C (475°F), Gas Mark 9. Place 1 pizza dough ball on the base only of a well-floured, 23 cm (9 inch) loose-bottomed tart tin. Push down on the dough with your fingertips, pressing it out to fill the base, leaving the border slightly thicker. If you get any tears, forcefully pinch the dough around the hole back together.

Spoon 2 tablespoons of the passata mixture over the base, top with a quarter of the aubergines, then scatter with a quarter each of the cheeses. Brush the border with oil, to glaze. Remove the heated baking sheet from the oven, slide the tin on to it, then quickly return to the oven. Bake for 7–8 minutes until crisp and risen. Serve immediately, garnished with basil leaves. As the first pizza cooks, prepare the next for the oven.

For courgette & smoked mozzarella pizza, replace the aubergines with 4 courgettes and griddle as above. Omit the ricotta and mozzarella and replace with 150 g (5 oz) sliced smoked mozzarella.

barley, bean & porcini soup

Serves **4**

Preparation time **10 minutes**, plus soaking

Cooking time **1 hour 35 minutes**

100 g (3½ oz) **dried borlotti beans**

100 g (3½ oz) **dried cannellini beans**

2 litres (3½ pints) **vegetable** or **chicken stock**

2 **celery sticks**, cubed

1 large **carrot**, cubed

1 **onion**, cubed

1 **bay leaf**

¼ teaspoon **crushed dried chillies**

75 g (3 oz) **pearl barley**

20 g (¾ oz) **dried porcini mushrooms**

2 tablespoons roughly chopped **flat leaf parsley**

salt and **pepper**

To serve

freshly grated **Parmesan cheese**

extra virgin olive oil

Put the dried beans in a large bowl, cover with cold water and leave to soak overnight.

Drain the soaked beans, put in a large saucepan and cover with the stock. Stir in the vegetables, bay leaf and crushed chillies and bring to the boil. Reduce the heat and skim off any scum that has risen to the surface. Simmer, uncovered, for 1 hour.

Stir the pearl barley and porcini into the pan and quickly return to the boil. Skim off any scum, reduce the heat and simmer for a further 30 minutes, or until the beans and barley are very tender.

Add the parsley, then check the seasoning, adding salt and pepper to taste. Serve with a scattering of grated Parmesan and a light drizzle of extra virgin olive oil.

For borlotti, pasta & red mullet soup, soak 200 g (7 oz) dried borlotti beans in cold water overnight, then cook with the stock, vegetables, bay leaves and crushed chillies, as in the second step above, increasing the cooking time to 1½ hours. Increase the heat to a rapid boil and stir in 150 g (5 oz) dried small pasta shapes. Cook for 6 minutes, then add 250 g (8 oz) red mullet fillets, cut into 3.5 cm (1½ inch) pieces. Cook for a further 2 minutes, or until the pasta is al dente. Scatter with 2 tablespoons roughly chopped flat leaf parsley and drizzle with extra virgin olive oil to serve.

chestnut, rice & pancetta soup

Serves **4**
Preparation time **10 minutes**
Cooking time **35 minutes**

50 g (2 oz) **butter**
150 g (5 oz) **pancetta**, cubed
1 **onion**, finely chopped
200 g (7 oz) pack **vacuum-
   packed cooked chestnuts**
150 g (5 oz) **arborio,
   carnaroli** or **vialone nano**
   rice
500 ml (17 fl oz) **chicken
   stock**
150 ml (¼ pint) **milk**
salt and **pepper**

Melt half the butter in a saucepan over a medium heat. Add the pancetta and onion and cook for 10 minutes. Cut the chestnuts in half and add to the pan with the rice and stock. Bring to the boil, then reduce the heat and simmer for 20 minutes, or until most of the liquid has been absorbed and the rice is tender.

Heat the milk in a small saucepan until tepid, then stir into the rice with the remaining butter and season the dish with salt and pepper. Cover and leave to stand for 5 minutes before serving.

For fennel, rice & pancetta soup with garlic & anchovies, follow the recipe above, but replace the onion with 1 large fennel bulb, thinly sliced, omit the chestnuts and replace the milk with 5 tablespoons of the Garlic Anchovy Dip on page 32.

seafood & fregola soup

Serves **4**
Preparation time **20 minutes**
Cooking time **20 minutes**

1.5 litres (2½ pints) **fish stock**
250 g (8 oz) **dried fregola** or
   other **dried small pasta
   shape**
4 tablespoons **extra virgin
   olive oil**
150 g (5 oz) **cherry tomatoes**,
   halved
2 **garlic cloves**, sliced
3 **anchovy fillets in olive oil**,
   drained and roughly chopped
¼ teaspoon **crushed dried
   chillies**
100 ml (3½ fl oz) **dry white
   wine**
500 g (1 lb) **mussels**, cleaned
   (see page 7)
375 g (12 oz) **clams**, cleaned
   (see page 7)
300 g (10 oz) **squid rings**
12 **raw shelled king prawns**
4 tablespoons roughly
   chopped **flat leaf parsley**
salt (optional)

Bring the stock to the boil in a saucepan, add the pasta and cook for 14–16 minutes, or according to the packet instructions, until al dente.

Meanwhile, heat the oil in a large frying pan or wok over a low heat. Add the tomatoes, garlic, anchovies and crushed chillies and cook for 5 minutes, or until the anchovies have melted into the pan and you can smell the aroma of the garlic.

Pour in the wine, bring to the boil and boil for 1 minute. Add all the seafood and cook, stirring, for 4–5 minutes until the mussels and clams have opened. Discard any that remain closed.

Tip the seafood mixture into the pan with the pasta. Add the parsley, season with salt, if necessary, and stir well. Serve immediately.

For pancetta, potato & fregola soup, cook the pasta as above, but replace the fish stock with 1.5 litres (2½ pints) chicken or vegetable stock. Heat 1 tablespoon olive oil in a separate saucepan. Add 1 chopped onion, 2 sliced celery sticks and 100 g (3½ oz) cubed pancetta and cook over a low heat for 5 minutes. Add 300 g (10 oz) peeled, cubed potatoes and 100 ml (3½ fl oz) dry white wine. Cook for about 10 minutes until the potatoes are tender, then add this mixture to the pan with the pasta. Serve with a drizzle of extra virgin olive oil.

white bean soup

Serves **6**
Preparation time **35 minutes**
Cooking time **1 hour 10 minutes**

250 g (8 oz) **dried white beans**, such as haricot or cannellini, soaked overnight in cold water
chicken or **vegetable stock** (optional)
handful of **sage leaves**
75 ml (3 fl oz) **olive oil**
2 **garlic cloves**, finely chopped
2 tablespoons chopped **sage** or **rosemary**
salt and **pepper**

To garnish
roughly chopped **flat leaf parsley**
Toasted Garlic & Chilli Oil (optional)

Drain the beans and put in a flameproof casserole with a tight-fitting lid. Cover with stock or water to a depth of 5 cm (2 inches) above the beans and push in the sage leaves. Bring to the boil, then cover and bake in a preheated oven, 160°C (325°F), Gas Mark 3, for about 1 hour, or until tender. The beans may not take this long, depending on their freshness, so test after 40 minutes. Leave in their cooking liquid.

Put half the beans, the cooked sage leaves and all the cooking liquid into a food processor or blender and process until smooth. Pour the purée back into the casserole with the remaining beans. Add extra stock or water if too thick.

Heat the oil in a frying pan over a low heat. Add the garlic and cook, stirring, until soft and golden. Add the chopped sage or rosemary and cook, stirring, for 30 seconds. Stir into the soup and reheat until boiling, then simmer gently for 10 minutes. Season well with salt and pepper. Serve immediately, garnished with chopped parsley and drizzled with Toasted Garlic & Chilli Oil (see below), if liked.

For toasted garlic & chilli oil, to serve as an accompaniment, heat 75 ml (3 fl oz) olive oil in a frying pan. Add 4 thinly sliced garlic cloves and cook over a medium heat until golden (don't let it overbrown or it will become bitter), then stir in a large pinch of dried chilli flakes. Spoon the garlic and oil over the soup.

tomato & bread soup

Serves **4**
Preparation time **15 minutes**
Cooking time **40 minutes**

2 tablespoons **olive oil**
1 small **onion**, finely chopped
1 **celery stick**, thinly sliced
250 g (8 oz) **day-old rustic bread**, sliced and crusts removed
3 **garlic cloves**, crushed
1 kg (2 lb) **ripe tomatoes**, roughly chopped
1 litre (1¾ pints) **vegetable** or **chicken stock**
12 **cherry tomatoes**, halved
15 large **basil leaves**
extra virgin olive oil, for drizzling
salt

Heat the oil in a large, heavy-based saucepan over a low heat. Add the onion and celery and cook for 10 minutes until softened and translucent.

Meanwhile, lightly toast the bread until dried and just beginning to colour, then break it into chunks.

Add the garlic to the saucepan and cook, stirring, for 1 minute, then tip in the toasted bread and tomatoes and cook for 5 minutes until the bread disintegrates into the tomatoes. Stir in the stock and simmer gently for 15 minutes. Add the cherry tomatoes and half the basil and simmer for a further 5 minutes.

Season with salt, cover and leave to stand for 5 minutes. Drizzle with extra virgin olive oil and scatter with the remaining basil to serve.

For roasted tomato, bread & balsamic soup, put all the ingredients listed above, except for the bread, stock and extra virgin olive oil, in a roasting tin with 1 tablespoon balsamic vinegar. Drizzle with olive oil and season with salt and pepper. Roast in a preheated oven, 160°C (325°F), Gas Mark 3, for 45 minutes until thickened and caramelized. Bring the stock to the boil in a saucepan, stir in the roasted vegetables and return to the boil. Divide the toasted bread chunks between 4 soup bowls and spoon over the soup. Serve with an extra drizzle of balsamic vinegar.

ribollita

Serves **4**
Preparation time **15 minutes**
Cooking time **45 minutes**

625 g (1 ¼ lb) **cavolo nero**
  (black cabbage)
2 tablespoons **extra virgin**
  olive oil, plus extra for
  drizzling
2 **celery sticks**, diced
1 **onion**, thinly sliced
1 large **carrot**, finely chopped
400 g (13 oz) **potatoes**, finely
  diced
400 g (13 oz) can **plum**
  tomatoes, drained
400 g (13 oz) can **cannellini**
  beans, drained and rinsed
1 **bay leaf**
4 **thyme sprigs**
1.5 litres (2½ pints) **vegetable**
  or **chicken stock**
4 slices of **stale ciabatta**
  bread, torn into bite-sized
  pieces
salt and **pepper**

Remove the thick stalks of the cabbage by holding the stems with one hand and using the other hand to strip away the leaves. Discard the stalks and roughly shred the leaves.

Heat the oil in a saucepan over a low heat. Add the celery, onion and carrot and cook for 8–10 minutes until soft and translucent. Stir in the cabbage, potatoes, tomatoes, half the cannellini beans, the bay leaf and thyme, then pour in the stock, season with salt and pepper and bring to the boil. Reduce the heat and simmer, covered, for 30 minutes, until the vegetables are meltingly tender and the stock richly flavoured.

Use a potato masher or fork to mash the remaining beans, then add to the soup, stirring well. Add the bread and continue stirring while it soaks up the soup. The ribollita should be thick enough so that it can be eaten with a fork, but if it starts to look dry, add a little water. Serve with a generous drizzle of oil.

For spring ribollita, follow the recipe above, but omit the cabbage. Cut 1 courgette into cubes and 100 g (3½ oz) French beans into 3.5 cm (1½ inch) pieces, then stir into the pan after the stock has come to the boil, together with 100 g (3½ oz) shelled broad beans. Complete the recipe as above.

radicchio risotto with pancetta

Serves **4**
Preparation time **10 minutes**
Cooking time **40 minutes**

4 slices of **pancetta**
50 g (2 oz) **salted butter**
1 **onion**, finely chopped
2 **garlic cloves**, finely chopped
200 g (7 oz) **arborio,**
　carnaroli or **vialone**
　nano rice
400 ml (14 fl oz) **Barolo** or
　other full-bodied red wine
175 g (6 oz) **radicchio**, sliced
600 ml (1 pint) **vegetable** or
　chicken stock, simmering
3 tablespoons freshly grated
　Parmesan cheese, plus
　extra to serve

Cook the pancetta on a baking sheet in a preheated oven, 200°C (400°F), Gas Mark 6, for 5–6 minutes, or until golden brown. Set aside.

Melt half the butter in a heavy-based saucepan over a low heat. Add the onion and cook for 10 minutes until softened. Add the garlic and rice and cook, stirring, for 1 minute. Pour in half the wine and cook, stirring, until absorbed. Add the remaining wine and cook, stirring, until absorbed.

Stir in the radicchio and 3 ladlefuls of the simmering stock. Slowly simmer, stirring constantly, until the stock has been absorbed and the rice parts when a wooden spoon is run through it. Add another ladleful of stock and continue to cook, stirring and adding the stock in ladlefuls, for 18–20 minutes until the rice is creamy and almost tender to the bite.

Remove from the heat and add the remaining butter and the Parmesan. Stir vigorously for 15 seconds. Cover with a tight-fitting lid and leave to stand for 1 minute. Serve immediately topped with the pancetta, with extra Parmesan on the side.

For watercress & lemon risotto, follow the recipe above from the second step, replacing the red wine with 200 ml (7 fl oz) dry white wine, omitting the radicchio and using 900 ml (1½ pints) simmering vegetable stock. Once the risotto is cooked, stir in 125 g (4 oz) roughly chopped watercress and the finely grated rind of 1 lemon with the butter and Parmesan. Leave to stand, as above, before serving.

tomatoes stuffed with rice

Serves **4**

Preparation time **15 minutes**, plus standing

Cooking time **35 minutes**

4 large or 8 small **tomatoes**, about 625 g (1 ¼ lb) in total

2 **garlic cloves**, crushed

75 g (3 oz) **arborio**, **carnaroli** or **vialone nano rice**

6 **basil leaves**, torn

2 tablespoons **extra virgin olive oil**, plus extra for oiling and drizzling

salt and **pepper**

Cut a slice off the stalk end of each tomato and set aside to use as lids. Scoop the pulp out of the tomatoes and chop. Transfer to a large bowl, taking care not to lose any of the tomato juices, and add the garlic, rice and basil. Season with salt and pepper and stir in 1 tablespoon of the oil. Cover and leave to stand at room temperature for 1 hour, for the rice to soak up all the juices.

Stuff the tomatoes with the rice mixture, then transfer to an oiled baking dish. Top with their reserved lids and drizzle with the remaining oil. Bake in a preheated oven, 180°C (350°F), Gas Mark 4, for 35 minutes until the tomatoes are soft and the rice is cooked through. Serve warm or at room temperature.

For tomatoes stuffed with rice, capers, anchovies & olives, prepare the tomatoes as above. For the filling, add 1 tablespoon each chopped flat leaf parsley, pitted black olives and rinsed capers in brine to the chopped tomato pulp with the garlic and rice. Toss in 2 drained, chopped anchovy fillets in olive oil and season with pepper only. Complete the recipe as above.

asparagus, pea & mint risotto

Serves **4**

Preparation time **10 minutes**

Cooking time **45 minutes**

500 g (1 lb) **asparagus spears**

1 litre (1¾ pints) **vegetable** or **fish stock**

50 g (2 oz) **butter**

1 **onion**, finely chopped

300 g (10 oz) **arborio, carnaroli** or **vialone nano rice**

150 ml (¼ pint) **dry white wine**

100 g (3½ oz) shelled **fresh** or **frozen peas**

4 tablespoons freshly grated **Parmesan cheese**, plus extra to serve

handful of **mint leaves**, roughly chopped

Cut the asparagus in half, at an angle, separating the tips from the thicker stalks. Reserve the tips. Put the stalks in a saucepan with the stock and bring to the boil. Boil for 5 minutes, then reduce the heat to a simmer. Remove the asparagus with a slotted spoon and process in a food processor or blender until puréed.

Melt half the butter in a heavy-based saucepan over a low heat. Add the onion and cook for 10 minutes until softened. Add the rice and cook, stirring, for 1 minute. Add the wine and cook, stirring, until absorbed. Stir in the puréed asparagus.

Add 2 ladlefuls of the simmering stock. Slowly simmer, stirring constantly, until the stock has been absorbed and the rice parts when a wooden spoon is run through it. Add another ladleful of stock and continue to cook, stirring and adding the stock in ladlefuls, reserving 2 ladlefuls, for 16–18 minutes until the rice is creamy and almost tender to the bite.

Add the peas and the reserved asparagus tips and stock and continue cooking until the stock is almost absorbed. Remove from the heat and stir in the Parmesan, mint and remaining butter. Stir vigorously for 15 seconds. Cover with a tight-fitting lid and leave to stand for 2 minutes. Serve immediately with extra Parmesan on the side.

For asparagus & pancetta risotto, follow the recipe above, but cook 150 g (5 oz) cubed pancetta with the onion. Omit the peas and replace the mint with 2 tablespoons roughly chopped flat leaf parsley.

saffron risotto

Serves **4**
Preparation time **5 minutes**
Cooking time **35 minutes**

50 g (2 oz) **butter**
1 **onion**, finely chopped
300 g (10 oz) **arborio**,
   carnaroli or **vialone**
   nano rice
150 ml (¼ pint) **dry white wine**
1 litre (1¾ pints) **beef** or
   vegetable stock, simmering
½ teaspoon **saffron threads**
4 tablespoons freshly grated
   Parmesan cheese, plus
   extra to serve

Melt half the butter in a heavy-based saucepan over a low heat. Add the onion and cook for 10 minutes until softened. Add the rice and cook, stirring, for 1 minute. Pour in the wine and cook, stirring, until absorbed.

Add 2 ladlefuls of the simmering stock and the saffron. Slowly simmer, stirring constantly, until the stock has been absorbed and the rice parts when a wooden spoon is run through it. Add another ladleful of stock and continue to cook, stirring and adding the stock in ladlefuls, for 18–20 minutes until the rice is creamy and almost tender to the bite.

Remove from the heat and stir in the Parmesan and remaining butter. Stir vigorously for 15 seconds. Cover with a tight-fitting lid and leave to stand for 1 minute. Serve immediately with extra Parmesan on the side.

For prawn, courgette & saffron risotto, follow the recipe above, but when the rice has been cooking for 15 minutes and most of the stock has been incorporated, stir 1 roughly grated courgette and 16 raw shelled king prawns into the rice mixture. Continue adding the remaining stock and complete the recipe as above, but omit the Parmesan.

baked polenta with gorgonzola

Serves **4**
Preparation time **5 minutes**
Cooking time **15 minutes**

750 ml (1 ¼ pints) **water**
225 g (7 ½ oz) **instant polenta**
50 g (2 oz) **butter**, plus extra
   for greasing
200 g (7 oz) **Gorgonzola**
   cheese, broken into pieces
5 tablespoons freshly grated
   Parmesan cheese
10 **cherry tomatoes**
salt and **pepper**

Bring the measurement water to the boil in a large, heavy-based saucepan. Set aside 2 tablespoons of the polenta to use for the topping and put the remaining polenta in a jug. Pour into the water in a slow but steady stream, stirring vigorously with a wooden spoon to prevent any lumps forming. Reduce the heat to a slow simmer and cook, stirring frequently, for about 5 minutes, or until the polenta is thick and comes away from the side of the pan. Stir in the butter and season with salt and pepper.

Pour half the polenta into a greased baking dish, about 25 x 18 cm (10 x 7 inches). Top with the Gorgonzola and half the Parmesan. Cover with the remaining cooked polenta, then top with the tomatoes. Stir the remaining Parmesan into the reserved uncooked polenta for the topping and scatter over the dish.

Cook under a preheated medium grill for 4–5 minutes until the tomatoes are slightly softened and beginning to char. Serve steaming hot.

For griddled herbed polenta, cook the polenta as in the first step, then stir in 2 tablespoons each roughly chopped flat leaf parsley, basil and wild rocket leaves and add 4 tablespoons grated Parmesan cheese. Tip into a 1 kg (2 lb) loaf tin and leave to cool at room temperature. Turn the polenta out and cut into 1 cm (½ inch) slices. Brush with olive oil, then cook on a preheated ridged griddle pan over a high heat for 1 minute on each side.

polenta chips

Serves **4**

Preparation time **15 minutes**, plus chilling

Cooking time **35 minutes**

50 g (2 oz) **butter**
600 ml (1 pint) **water**
1 teaspoon **salt**
125 g (4 oz) **instant polenta**
sunflower oil, for oiling and deep-frying
plain flour, for coating
paprika, for sprinkling
salt

Put the butter, measurement water and salt in a heavy-based saucepan and bring to the boil. Put the polenta in a jug and pour into the water mixture in a slow but steady stream, stirring vigorously with a wooden spoon to prevent lumps forming. Reduce the heat to a slow simmer and cook, stirring frequently, for about 5 minutes, or until the polenta is thick and comes away from the side of the pan.

Transfer the polenta to a shallow oiled dish, smooth the top and leave to cool. Cover and chill until firm.

Turn the polenta out on to wet greaseproof paper and cut into thick chips with a wet knife.

Heat enough oil for deep-frying in a deep saucepan to 180–190°C (350–375°F), or until a cube of bread browns in 30 seconds. Roll the chips in a little flour to coat, add to the hot oil, in batches, and cook for 6–8 minutes until pale golden brown and crisp. Remove with a slotted spoon and drain on kitchen paper. Sprinkle with salt and paprika. Keep warm in a low oven with the door ajar until ready to serve.

For tomato & basil dip, to serve as an accompaniment, blend 4 ripe tomatoes with 1 garlic clove, 4 basil leaves and ½ deseeded red chilli. Stir in 2 tablespoons extra virgin olive oil and season with salt. Serve with the chips, omitting the paprika.

cheesy polenta & mushrooms

Serves **4**

Preparation time **10 minutes**

Cooking time **15 minutes**

400 g (13 oz) **mixed wild mushrooms**, such as porcini, girolles and chanterelles
25 g (1 oz) **butter**
2 **garlic cloves**, chopped
5 whole **sage leaves**
50 ml (2 fl oz) **dry vermouth**
salt and **pepper**

Polenta
750 ml (1¼ pints) **water**
200 g (7 oz) **instant polenta**
50 g (2 oz) **Parmesan cheese**, freshly grated
50 g (2 oz) **butter**, cubed

Brush away any soil and grit from the mushrooms with a moist cloth, then slice the porcini and tear any other large mushrooms in half. Set aside.

Melt the butter in a large frying pan over a medium-high heat. Add the garlic, sage and the dense, tougher mushrooms and cook for 2–3 minutes. Add the remaining mushrooms, season with salt and pepper and cook for 2–3 minutes until soft and cooked through. Pour in the vermouth and cook, stirring, for 1 minute.

For the polenta, bring the measurement water to the boil in a large, heavy-based saucepan. Put the polenta in a jug and pour into the water in a slow but steady stream, stirring vigorously with a wooden spoon to prevent any lumps forming. Reduce the heat to a slow simmer and cook, stirring frequently, for about 5 minutes, or until the polenta is thick and comes away from the side of the pan. Stir in the butter and season with salt and pepper.

Divide the polenta between 4 serving plates, then top with the mushrooms.

For cheesy polenta with mushrooms & tomato, cook the mushrooms as above, but replace the rosemary with 3 chopped thyme sprigs and use 150 ml (¼ pint) full-bodied red wine instead of the vermouth. When the wine has boiled for 1 minute, stir in 300 ml (½ pint) passata. Season with salt and pepper and bring to the boil, then simmer for 5 minutes. Cook the polenta as above, then gradually stir in the cheese. Serve with the mushroom and tomato mixture.

red mullet with salsa verde

Serves **4**
Preparation time **20 minutes**
Cooking time **10 minutes**

4 **red mullet**, gutted and
    scaled
2 tablespoons **olive oil**
1 **lemon**, halved lengthways
    and thinly sliced
salt and **pepper**

Salsa verde
2 **garlic cloves**, finely chopped
3 **anchovy fillets in olive oil**,
    finely chopped
1 tablespoon **capers in brine**,
    rinsed and finely chopped
4 tablespoons roughly
    chopped **flat leaf parsley**
2 tablespoons roughly
    chopped **mint**
2 tablespoons roughly
    chopped **basil**
1 tablespoon **red wine
    vinegar**
4 tablespoons **extra virgin
    olive oil**

Combine all the ingredients for the salsa verde in a
bowl and season with salt and pepper. Set aside.

Wash the inside and outside of the mullet under cold
running water and pat dry with kitchen paper. Cut
2–3 deep slashes along the width of both sides of the
mullet, then brush the fish all over with the oil. Season
with salt and pepper. Insert a lemon slice into each
slash, then tuck a couple of slices inside each fish.

Lay the mullet on a nonstick baking sheet and
cook under a preheated very high grill, about 10 cm
(4 inches) from the heat source, for about 5 minutes
on each side until cooked through and lightly charred.
Serve immediately with the salsa verde.

**For smoked mackerel with potato & salsa verde
salad**, boil or steam 500 g (1 lb) baby new potatoes
until tender, then lightly crush with the back of a
spoon. Prepare the salsa verde as above, but using
5 tablespoons extra virgin olive oil. Toss the warm
potatoes with the dressing. Replace the red mullet
with 4 smoked mackerel fillets. Break into large flakes
and gently toss into the salad.

roast garlic-studded monkfish

Serves **4**

Preparation time **20 minutes**, plus marinating

Cooking time **30 minutes**

1 kg (2 lb) **monkfish tail**, trimmed and boned

3–4 **bay leaves**

1 teaspoon **fennel seeds**

4 **garlic cloves**, cut into thick slivers

4 tablespoons **olive oil**

a few **thyme sprigs**

2 **red peppers**, cored, deseeded and roughly chopped

1 **aubergine**, cut into bite-sized chunks

2 **courgettes**, cut into bite-sized chunks

3 **ripe plum tomatoes**, cut into chunks

3 tablespoons **lemon juice**

salt and **pepper**

To garnish

2 tablespoons **salted capers**, rinsed and chopped

3 tablespoons chopped **flat leaf parsley**

Lay the bay leaves over one monkfish fillet and scatter over the fennel seeds. Lay the other fillet on top and tie at 2.5 cm (1 inch) intervals with fine string. With the tip of a sharp knife, make slits all over the monkfish and push in the garlic slivers. Put the oil, thyme and a little pepper into a glass dish, add the monkfish and turn well to coat. Cover and leave to marinate in the refrigerator for at least 2 hours or overnight.

Remove from the marinade. Pour 2 tablespoons of the marinade into a heavy, nonstick frying pan and heat until almost smoking. Add the monkfish and cook, turning, for 2–3 minutes until sealed. Set aside.

Heat the remaining marinade in the pan. Add the vegetables and quickly brown. Transfer to a heavy, shallow baking dish, set the monkfish on top and add the tomatoes and lemon juice. Bake in a preheated oven, 220°C (425°F), Gas Mark 7, for 20 minutes, basting and turning the vegetables occasionally.

Remove the string and cut the fish into thick slices. Season the vegetables with salt and pepper. Serve the monkfish on the vegetables, garnished with the capers and parsley.

For roasted monkfish with olive paste, omit the marinade. Make a quick olive paste by blending 100 g (3½ oz) pitted black olives, the leaves from 2 sprigs thyme, 1 garlic clove and 3 tablespoons olive oil. Spread over one monkfish fillet then lay the other fillet on top and tie as above. Seal the monkfish in a pan with 2 tablespoons olive oil then roast it with the vegetables, as above.

sole with tomatoes & capers

Serves **2**
Preparation time **10 minutes**
Cooking time **25 minutes**

4 tablespoons **olive oil**
1 **garlic clove**, roughly
 chopped
2 **Dover sole**, about 400 g
 (13 oz) each, skinned
 (ask your fishmonger to do
 this for you)
50 g (2 oz) **plain flour**,
 seasoned with **salt**
100 ml (3½ fl oz) **dry
 white wine**
200 ml (7 fl oz) **passata**
pinch of **caster sugar**
½ teaspoon **dried oregano**
2 tablespoons **capers in
 brine**, rinsed
salt and **pepper** (optional)

Heat the oil in a large frying pan over a low heat. Add the garlic and cook for 10 minutes. Discard the garlic and increase the heat to high.

Pat the sole dry with kitchen paper, then turn in the seasoned flour to coat both sides. Gently lower into the hot oil and cook for 4—5 minutes on each side until golden (if your pan isn't large enough, cook individually and keep the cooked sole warm in a low oven while you cook the remaining fish). Remove to a warmed serving plate.

Pour the wine into the frying pan and cook, stirring well with a wooden spoon to loosen any sediment from the base of the pan, for 1 minute. Add the passata, sugar, oregano and capers and bring to the boil. Check the seasoning and add salt and pepper if necessary, then spoon the sauce over the fish. Serve immediately.

For sole with lemon, parsley & garlic, cook the sole as above and keep warm. Melt 50 g (2 oz) butter in the frying pan over a medium heat and stir in the grated rind of 1 lemon and 2 crushed garlic cloves. Cook for 2 minutes, then remove from the heat and stir in the juice of 1 lemon and 2 tablespoons finely chopped flat leaf parsley. Spoon over the fish and serve immediately.

sardines stuffed with fennel

Serves **4**

Preparation time **15 minutes**, plus cooling

Cooking time **25 minutes**

4 tablespoons **extra virgin olive oil**

1 **fennel bulb**, thinly sliced

1 **onion**, thinly sliced

pared **rind** of 1 small **orange**

pared **rind** of 1 **lemon**

1 tablespoon roughly chopped **dill**

1 teaspoon **fennel seeds**

¼ teaspoon **crushed dried chillies**

2 **garlic cloves**, finely chopped

5 tablespoons **fresh white breadcrumbs**

2 tablespoons roughly chopped **flat leaf parsley**

4 large or 8 small **sardines**, filleted

juice of ½ **lemon**

salt

lemon wedges, to serve

Pour half the oil into a large, heavy-based frying pan and stir in the fennel and onion. Add the citrus rind, dill, fennel seeds and crushed chillies and place the pan over a very low heat. Cook, stirring frequently, for 12–15 minutes until the fennel and onion are golden and caramelized, being careful not to burn. Add the garlic and cook, stirring, for 2 minutes. Remove from the heat and stir in half the breadcrumbs and parsley. Season with salt and leave to cool.

Drizzle 1 tablespoon of the remaining oil over a large baking sheet. Add half the sardine fillets, skin-side down. Season lightly with salt, then spread the fennel mixture over each fillet. Press a second fillet on top, skin-side up, and scatter with the remaining breadcrumbs and parsley. Drizzle with the remaining oil and squeeze the lemon juice over the fish. Season again with salt.

Cook under a preheated high grill for 6–8 minutes until the fish is opaque all the way through. Serve with lemon wedges, accompanied by a tomato and lettuce salad.

For spaghetti with sardine & fennel sauce, cook 400 g (13 oz) dried spaghetti in a large saucepan of salted boiling water for 8–10 minutes, or according to the packet instructions, until al dente. Meanwhile, follow the first step above, omitting the breadcrumbs and adding 250 g (8 oz) roughly chopped sardine fillets to the pan with the garlic. Cook for 2 minutes until cooked through. Drain the pasta, return to the pan and stir through the sauce.

swordfish with onion & sultanas

Serves **4**
Preparation time **10 minutes**
Cooking time **20 minutes**

4 tablespoons **olive oil**
1 **onion**, thinly sliced
1 **celery stick**, sliced
2 tablespoons **sultanas**
1 **bay leaf**
3 tablespoons **pine nuts**
2 **garlic cloves**, sliced
4 **swordfish steaks**, about
 2.5 cm (1 inch) thick
plain flour, seasoned with **salt**
 and **pepper**, for coating
150 ml (¼ pint) **dry**
 white wine

Heat half the oil in a large, heavy-based frying pan over a low heat. Add the onion, celery, sultanas and bay leaf and cook for 8–10 minutes until soft and golden. Stir in the pine nuts and garlic and cook for a further 2 minutes. Remove to a dish.

Heat the remaining oil in the pan over a high heat. Turn the swordfish steaks in the seasoned flour to coat on both sides. Add to the hot oil and cook for 3 minutes on each side until golden brown.

Return the onion mixture to the pan and pour in the wine. Boil vigorously for 2 minutes. Serve immediately.

For tuna with onion & olives, follow the first step above, but omit the sultanas and replace the pine nuts with 50 g (2 oz) halved, pitted black olives. Continue with the recipe as above, but use 4 tuna steaks, about 2.5 cm (1 inch) thick, instead of the swordfish steaks.

mussels alla marinara

Serves **4**
Preparation time **15 minutes**
Cooking time **10 minutes**

3 tablespoons **olive oil**
4 **garlic cloves**, chopped
150 ml (¼ pint) **dry
white wine**
400 g (13 oz) can **chopped
tomatoes**
1 small **red chilli**, deseeded
and finely chopped
2 tablespoons chopped **flat
leaf parsley**, plus extra
whole leaves to garnish
2 kg (4 lb) **mussels**, cleaned
(see page 7)
salt and **pepper**

Heat the oil in a large saucepan over a low heat. Add the garlic and cook for about 5 minutes until golden. Add the wine, tomatoes, chilli and chopped parsley and bring to the boil. Season well with salt and pepper.

Add the mussels to the pan, cover and cook over a high heat, shaking the pan frequently, for 4–5 minutes, or until the shells have opened. Stir well and discard any that remain closed.

Scatter the whole parsley leaves over the mussels and serve immediately with crusty bread, if liked.

For squid alla marinara, fry the garlic as above, also adding ½ teaspoon fennel seeds to the pan. Continue following the recipe, replacing the mussels with 500 g (1 lb) squid rings.

fried calamari

Serves **4**
Preparation time **15 minutes**
Cooking time **10 minutes**

1 kg (2 lb) **squid**, cleaned
    (see page 7)
vegetable oil, for deep-frying
75 g (3 oz) **plain flour**
salt
lemon wedges, to serve

Cut the squid bodies into rings. Dry the rings and the tentacles thoroughly with kitchen paper.

Heat enough oil for deep-frying in a deep saucepan to 180–190°C (350–375°F), or until a cube of bread browns in 30 seconds. Season the squid with salt, then coat half in the flour, shaking off any excess. Add to the hot oil and cook for 2–3 minutes, or until golden and crisp. Remove with a slotted spoon and drain on kitchen paper. Scatter with a pinch of salt. Repeat with the remaining squid. Serve immediately with lemon wedges.

For spicy fried prawns, replace the squid with 20 raw peeled king prawns. Mix ¼ teaspoon cayenne pepper into 100 g (3½ oz) plain flour and make into a batter by stirring in 175 ml (6 fl oz) ice-cold sparkling water. Season the prawns with salt, then coat in the batter and deep-fry in batches, as above, for 4–5 minutes. Drain on kitchen paper and serve with lemon wedges.

classic meatloaf

Serves **4**

Preparation time **25 minutes**

Cooking time **55 minutes**

2 thick slices of **white bread**,
    crusts removed and broken
    into chunks

2 tablespoons **milk**

large pinch of freshly
    grated **nutmeg**

500 g (1 lb) **minced beef**

6 slices of **pancetta** or
    streaky bacon,
    finely chopped

1 small **onion**, finely chopped

3 **garlic cloves**, finely chopped

4 tablespoons freshly grated
    Parmesan cheese

1 **egg**, lightly beaten

100 g (3½ oz) **fine dry
    white breadcrumbs**

2 tablespoons **olive oil**

150 ml (¼ pint) **dry
    white wine**

400 g (13 oz) can **chopped
    tomatoes**

finely grated **rind** of 1 **orange**

2 tablespoons roughly
    chopped **flat leaf parsley**

salt and **pepper**

Soak the bread in a bowl with the milk and nutmeg for about 10 minutes until the milk is absorbed. Mash with a fork. Combine the beef, pancetta or bacon, onion and half the garlic in a large bowl. Add the Parmesan, egg and bread. Season with salt and pepper. Mix gently with your hands until well combined. Form into a loaf shape. Spread the breadcrumbs out on a large plate and roll the meatloaf over to coat thoroughly.

Heat the oil in a shallow saucepan with a tight-fitting lid over a medium heat. Add the meatloaf and cook, turning occasionally, until golden all over. Add the wine, boil rapidly until reduced by half, then add the tomatoes. Cover and simmer very gently, turning the meatloaf occasionally and adding a little water if necessary, for 40–45 minutes, or until a knife inserted into the centre comes out hot.

Lift on to a serving dish. Stir the orange rind, parsley and remaining garlic into the pan and simmer for 2 minutes. Season with salt and pepper. Spoon over the meatloaf.

For meatballs in red wine sauce, soak the bread, then combine the remaining ingredients as above, omitting the breadcrumbs, oil, wine and tomatoes. Season and shape into golf-ball sized balls. Heat 2 tablespoons olive oil in a frying pan over a medium heat, add the meatballs and cook for 8–10 minutes until golden. Add 200 ml (7 fl oz) full-bodied red wine, boil for 2 minutes, then stir in the tomatoes. Bring to the boil, then simmer, covered, for 20 minutes.

calves' liver & caramelized onions

Serves **4**

Preparation time **10 minutes**

Cooking time **40–45 minutes**

50 g (2 oz) **butter**

2 tablespoons **olive oil**

2 large **onions**, thinly sliced

625 g (1 ¼ 1b) **calves' liver**, thinly sliced (ask your butcher to slice as thinly as possible)

2 tablespoons finely chopped **flat leaf parsley**

salt and **pepper**

Melt half the butter with the oil in a large frying pan with a tight-fitting lid. Add the onions and season with salt and pepper, then cover and cook over a very low heat, stirring occasionally, for 35–40 minutes until very soft and golden. Remove to a bowl and increase the heat under the pan to high.

Season the liver with salt and pepper and melt the remaining butter in the pan. Once the butter starts foaming, add the liver and cook for 1–2 minutes until browned. Turn over and return the onions to the pan. Cook for a further minute, then serve immediately with the parsley scattered over.

For chicken liver & caramelized onions, cook the onions as above and remove from the pan. Replace the calves' liver with 400 g (13 oz) chicken livers, coated in seasoned flour. Cook the livers in the remaining butter in the pan as above for 4–5 minutes, turning once. Add 1 tablespoon aged balsamic vinegar, swirl in the pan for a couple of seconds, then return the caramelized onions to the pan. Cook for a further minute, stir in the parsley as above and serve immediately.

roast lamb with wine & juniper

Serves **6**
Preparation time **20 minutes**
Cooking time **1 hour**
  35 minutes

2 tablespoons **olive oil**
1 **leg of lamb**, about 1.5 kg
  (3 lb), trimmed of excess fat
10 **juniper berries**, crushed
3 **garlic cloves**, crushed
50 g (2 oz) **salted anchovies**,
  boned and rinsed
1 tablespoon chopped
  rosemary
2 tablespoons **balsamic
  vinegar**
2 **rosemary sprigs**
300 ml (½ pint) **dry white
  wine**
salt and **pepper**

Heat the oil in a roasting tin in which the lamb will fit snugly. Add the lamb and cook until browned all over. Leave to cool.

Pound 6 of the juniper berries, the garlic, anchovies and chopped rosemary with the end of a rolling pin in a bowl. Stir in the vinegar and mix to a paste. Make small incisions all over the lamb with a small, sharp knife. Spread the paste over the lamb, working it into the incisions. Season with salt and pepper. Put the rosemary sprigs in the roasting tin and put the lamb on top. Pour in the wine and add the remaining juniper berries.

Cover the roasting tin with foil and bring to the boil, then cook in a preheated oven, 160°C (325°F), Gas Mark 3, for 1 hour, turning the lamb every 20 minutes. Raise the temperature to 200°C (400°F), Gas Mark 6, uncover and roast for a further 30 minutes until the lamb is very tender.

For leg of lamb with lemon & rosemary, omit the juniper berries and pound the grated zest of 2 lemons, with the garlic, anchovies and rosemary. Replace the vinegar with the juice of 1 lemon. Spoon the sauce over the lamb, as above.

pork braised in milk

Serves **6**
Preparation time **10 minutes**,
   plus resting
Cooking time **1¾ hours**

25 g (1 oz) **butter**
3 tablespoons **olive oil**
1 **loin of pork with 6 chops**,
   about 2.25 kg (4½ lb) in
   total, chined and skin
   removed (ask your butcher
   to do this for you)
1 litre (1¾ pints) **milk**
4 **garlic cloves**, peeled but
   kept whole
pared **rind** of 2 **lemons**
8 **sage leaves**
salt and **pepper**

Melt the butter with the oil in a large, heavy-based flameproof casserole or a roasting tin large enough to hold the pork. Season the pork with salt and pepper and add to the pan, fat-side down. Cook over a medium-high heat for 10 minutes until golden brown.

Pour away most of the fat and turn the pork over, skin-side up. Pour in the milk and add the garlic, lemon rind and sage. Bring to the boil, then cover with a lid or foil, leaving a little gap for the steam to escape. Cook on the hob over a very low heat or in a preheated oven, 150°C (300°F), Gas Mark 2, for 1½ hours, basting regularly with the sauce. The pork is ready when the meat feels very tender when pierced with a fork.

Remove the meat and leave to rest for 10 minutes. The sauce, which should be biscuit in colour, will be unattractively lumpy, so vigorously whisk to break up the lumps or process in a food processor or blender until smooth. Reheat if necessary and season with salt and pepper. Separate the loin into 6 chops and serve with the sauce spooned over.

For lamb shanks braised in milk, replace the pork with 6 lamb shanks and cook as above, using 3 rosemary sprigs instead of the sage leaves. Add a generous grating of nutmeg to the sauce before whisking or blending away the lumps.

lamb cutlets with red pesto

Serves **4**

Preparation time **15 minutes**,
  plus marinating

Cooking time **4–6 minutes**

12 **lamb cutlets**, each
  approximately 100 g (3½ oz)
2 tablespoons **olive oil**
juice of ½ **lemon**
1 **garlic clove**, crushed
2 **rosemary sprigs**, roughly
  chopped
salt and **pepper**

Pesto
50 g (2 oz) **sunblush
  tomatoes**
75 g (3 oz) **bottled roasted
  peppers**
50 g (2 oz) **blanched
  almonds**
½ **red chilli**, halved and
  deseeded
2 **garlic cloves**, crushed
3 tablespoons freshly grated
  Parmesan cheese
3 tablespoons **extra virgin
  olive oil**

Put the cutlets in a bowl with the oil, lemon juice, garlic and rosemary and toss well to combine. Cover and leave to marinate in the refrigerator for at least 1 hour or up to overnight.

Meanwhile, for the pesto, put the tomatoes, peppers, almonds, chilli and garlic in a food processor and process to a paste. Stir in the Parmesan and oil and season with salt.

Season the marinated cutlets with salt and pepper. Heat a ridged griddle pan over a high heat until smoking hot, or preheat a gas barbecue to high or, if using a charcoal barbecue, get the coals to the stage where there are no more flames and the coals are covered with a thin layer of grey ash. Add the cutlets and cook for 2–3 minutes on each side, depending on whether you like your lamb pink in the centre or well done. Serve with the red pesto on the side.

For a steak sandwich with red pesto, replace the lamb with 500 g (1 lb) fillet steak. Marinate and cook as above, then slice. Meanwhile, make the red pesto as above. Cut 4 ciabatta rolls open and drizzle the inside with olive oil. Griddle or barbecue for a few seconds to char slightly. Put the beef slices in the rolls and top with wild rocket leaves, red pesto and a few slices of red onion.

devilled fillet steaks

Serves **4**

Preparation time **10 minutes**

Cooking time **10 minutes**

2 tablespoons **olive oil**

4 **fillet steaks**, about 175 g
(6 oz) each

2 tablespoons **balsamic
vinegar**

75 ml (3 fl oz) **full-bodied
red wine**

4 tablespoons **beef stock**

2 **garlic cloves**, chopped

1 teaspoon crushed
fennel seeds

1 tablespoon **sun-dried
tomato purée**

½ teaspoon **crushed
dried chillies**

salt and **pepper**

To garnish

chopped **flat leaf parsley**

wild rocket leaves (optional)

Heat the oil in a nonstick frying pan until smoking hot. Add the steaks and cook over a very high heat for about 2 minutes on each side, if you want your steaks to be medium rare. Remove to a plate, season with salt and pepper and keep warm in a low oven.

Pour the vinegar, wine and stock into the pan and boil for 30 seconds, scraping any sediment from the base of the pan. Add the garlic and fennel seeds and whisk in the sun-dried tomato purée and crushed chillies. Bring the sauce to the boil and boil fast to reduce until syrupy.

Transfer the steaks to warmed serving plates, pouring any collected meat juices into the sauce. Return the sauce to the boil, then season with salt and pepper.

Pour the sauce over the steaks and serve immediately, garnished with chopped parsley and wild rocket leaves, if liked. Slice the steaks before serving, if you wish.

For devilled chicken breasts, heat the oil and use to cook 4 skinned chicken breasts for 5 minutes on each side. Leaving the chicken in the pan, follow the recipe above, replacing the beef stock with 4 tablespoons chicken stock and using ½ teaspoon dried oregano instead of the fennel seeds.

rabbit in white wine & rosemary

Serves **4–6**
Preparation time **15 minutes**
Cooking time **2 hours**

25 g (1 oz) **butter**
3 tablespoons **olive oil**
1 **rabbit**, about 1.5 kg (3 lb),
    cut into joints (ask your
    butcher to do this for you)
2 **onions**, thinly sliced
1 small **celery stick**,
    finely diced
pinch of **crushed**
    dried chillies
3 large **rosemary sprigs**
1 **lemon**, quartered
12 **black olives**
350 ml (12 fl oz) **dry**
    white wine
250 ml (8 fl oz) **chicken stock**
salt

Melt half the butter with the oil in a large, flameproof casserole with a tight-fitting lid large enough to hold the rabbit in a single layer. Lightly season the rabbit with salt and add to the pan with the onions, celery, crushed chillies and rosemary. Cover and cook over a low heat for 1½ hours, turning the rabbit pieces every 30 minutes.

Uncover the pan, increase the heat to high and boil until most of the juices released by the rabbit during cooking have evaporated. Add the lemon and olives, stir well, then pour in the wine. Bring to the boil and boil for 2 minutes, for the alcohol to evaporate.

Pour in the stock and simmer, turning and basting the rabbit occasionally, for a further 10–12 minutes until you have a rich, syrupy sauce. Serve hot.

For chicken with olives & rosemary, replace the rabbit with 1 chicken, cut into 8 joints (ask your butcher to do this). Put the chicken with all the remaining ingredients above in a large roasting tin and roast in a preheated oven, 200°C (400°F), Gas Mark 6, for 1 hour, turning the chicken pieces occasionally, until the meat is tender and most of the juices have evaporated. Stir in 3 tablespoons double cream and serve immediately.

roast herbed pork belly

Serves **4–6**
Preparation time **15 minutes**, plus resting
Cooking time **1 hour 50 minutes**

10 **sage leaves**
2 large **rosemary sprigs**
3 **garlic cloves**, crushed
1 tablespoon **fennel seeds**
4 tablespoons **olive oil**
1 **boned pork belly joint**, about 1.25 kg (2½ lb)
salt and **pepper**

Roughly chop the sage and rosemary and combine with the garlic, fennel seeds and half the oil in a small bowl.

Place the pork on a chopping board, skin-side up, and score the rind at 2.5 cm (1 inch) intervals (the easiest way of doing this is with a Stanley knife). Turn the meat over, skin-side down, and season with salt and pepper. Rub the herb mixture all over the flesh. Roll the pork up and tie it tightly with string. Rub the skin all over with the remaining oil, then a generous amount of salt.

Roast in a preheated oven, 220°C (425°F), Gas Mark 7, for 20 minutes, then reduce the temperature to 160°C (325°F), Gas Mark 3, and roast for a further 1½ hours. Leave the meat to rest for 10 minutes before carving and serving. The Braised Black Cabbage & Borlotti on page 130 or the Braised Artichokes & Potatoes on page 122 would make great accompaniments for the pork.

For sausage & apricot stuffed pork, instead of the herb mixture, roughly chop 4 sage leaves and 6 ready-to-eat dried apricots, then stir into 150 g (5 oz) pork sausagemeat. Follow the recipe above from the second step onwards, spreading the sausagement mixture over the seasoned pork.

sausages & lentils in tomato sauce

Serves **4**

Preparation time **10 minutes**

Cooking time **1 hour 10 minutes**

3 tablespoons **olive oil**

8 **Italian pork sausages**

1 **onion**, roughly chopped

1 **celery stick**, roughly chopped

3 **garlic cloves**, crushed

200 ml (7 fl oz) **full-bodied red wine**

400 g (13 oz) can **chopped tomatoes**

1.2 litres (2 pints) **chicken stock**

1 **bay leaf**

1 **dried red chilli**

125 g (4 oz) **green lentils**

salt and **pepper**

extra virgin olive oil, for drizzling

Heat the oil in a large, heavy-based saucepan in which the sausages fit in a single layer. Add the sausages and cook over a medium heat for 10–12 minutes until golden brown all over. Remove and set aside.

Add the onion and celery to the pan and cook over a low heat for 8–10 minutes until softened. Stir in the garlic and cook for a further 2 minutes.

Increase the heat to high, pour in the wine and boil vigorously for 2 minutes, scraping any sediment from the base of the pan. Stir in the tomatoes, stock, bay leaf and chilli and bring to the boil. Add the lentils and return the sausages to the pan. Simmer gently for 40 minutes, or until the sausages and lentils are cooked through. Season with salt and pepper. Serve with a drizzle of extra virgin olive oil, accompanied by some crusty bread.

For cod & lentils in tomato sauce, omit the sausages and cook the other ingredients as above from the second step onwards, finally adding the lentils to the pan. Once cooked until tender, add 4 cod fillets, about 125 g (4 oz) each, to the pan and season with salt and pepper. Scatter with the grated rind of 1 lemon and 1 tablespoon chopped parsley, cover and cook over a low heat for 10–12 minutes until cooked through.

chicken milanese

Serves **4**
Preparation time **20 minutes**
Cooking time **10–25 minutes**

4 **boneless chicken breasts**,
   about 150–175 g (5–6 oz)
   each, skinned
100 g (3½ oz) **plain flour**
2 **eggs**, beaten
200 g (7 oz) **dry white**
   breadcrumbs
3 tablespoons **flat leaf**
   parsley, chopped
5 tablespoons **olive oil**
salt and **pepper**
lemon wedges, to serve

Lay the chicken breasts between 2 sheets of clingfilm and beat with a rolling pin until no more than 1 cm (½ inch) thick.

Put the flour, eggs and breadcrumbs in 3 separate dishes and season the flour and eggs with salt and pepper. Stir the chopped parsley into the breadcrumbs. Turn each chicken breast in the flour, then dip into the eggs and coat in the breadcrumbs.

Heat the oil in a frying pan over a high heat. Add the flattened chicken breasts, 1 or 2 at a time, and cook for 2–3 minutes on each side until golden. Remove with a slotted spoon and drain on kitchen paper. Serve with lemon wedges, accompanied by a crisp green salad.

For turkey Milanese, replace the chicken with 4 turkey breast steaks, about 150–175 g (5–6 oz) each, sliced 1 cm (½ inch) thick. For the coating, use 200 g (7 oz) fresh white breadcrumbs instead of the dry breadcrumbs and flavour with 2 crushed garlic cloves, 2 tablespoons chopped flat leaf parsley and 1 tablespoon chopped thyme. Follow the recipe above.

roast chicken with herbs & garlic

Serves **4**

Preparation time **10 minutes**

Cooking time **about 1 hour**

8 **garlic cloves**, unpeeled

4 large **thyme sprigs**

3 large **rosemary sprigs**

1 **organic** or **free-range chicken**, about 1.75 kg (3½ lb)

1 tablespoon **olive oil**

salt and **pepper**

Put the garlic cloves and half the herb sprigs in the body cavity of the chicken. Pat the chicken dry with kitchen paper and rub the oil all over the outside of the bird. Strip the leaves off the remaining herb sprigs and rub over the bird, with a little salt and pepper.

Place the chicken, breast-side up, in a roasting tin. Roast in a preheated oven, 220°C (425°F), Gas Mark 7, for 10 minutes. Turn the chicken over, breast-side down, reduce the oven temperature to 180°C (350°F), Gas Mark 4, and cook for a further 20 minutes. Finally, turn the chicken back to its original position and roast for another 25 minutes until the skin is crisp and golden. Check that the chicken is cooked by piercing the thigh with a knife. The juices should run clear, with no sign of pink. If not, cook for a further 10 minutes.

Transfer to a warmed serving plate and leave to rest for 5 minutes before serving with the pan juices.

For roast chicken with lemon & sage, cut a lemon in half, then cut 1 half into slices. Carefully lift the skin covering the breast meat and ease in the lemon slices. Put the other lemon half in the body cavity with 8 sage leaves, in place of the thyme and rosemary sprigs, and the garlic as above. Roast as above.

aubergine & courgette parmigiana

Serves **6**
Preparation time **15 minutes**
Cooking time **45–50 minutes**

500 ml (17 fl oz) **passata**
handful of **basil leaves**, torn
2 **garlic cloves**, crushed
4 tablespoons **olive oil**
1 kg (2 lb) **aubergines**, cut
  lengthways into 1 cm
  (½ inch) slices
500 g (1 lb) **courgettes**, cut
  lengthways into 1 cm
  (½ inch) slices
300 g (10 oz) **mozzarella
  cheese** (drained weight),
  chopped
100 g (3½ oz) **Parmesan
  cheese**, freshly grated
salt and **pepper**

Combine the passata, basil and garlic in a bowl, season with salt and pepper and stir in half the oil.

Toss the aubergines and courgettes in the remaining oil to coat. Heat a ridged griddle pan over a high heat until smoking hot. Add the vegetables, in batches, and cook for 2–3 minutes on each side until tender all the way through.

Spoon a little of the passata mixture on to the base of a deep baking dish, about 30 x 20 cm (12 x 8 inches). Cover with a layer of mixed aubergines and courgettes, then scatter with some of the mozzarella. Spoon over 4 tablespoons of the passata mixture and scatter with Parmesan. Continue layering in this way until all the ingredients are used up, finishing with a layer of passata mixture and Parmesan.

Bake in a preheated oven, 180°C (350°F), Gas Mark 4, for 25–30 minutes, or until golden and bubbly.

For fennel & olive parmigiana, replace the aubergines and courgettes with 4 fennel bulbs, cut lengthways into 1 cm (½ inch) slices and 1 large onion, sliced into rings. Griddle and layer with the passata mixture and cheese as above, then top the final layer with a scattering of 15 pitted black olives. Bake as above.

braised artichokes & potatoes

Serves **4**
Preparation time **30 minutes**
Cooking time **1 hour**

6 **baby globe artichokes**
juice of 1 **lemon**
4 tablespoons **olive oil**
2 **shallots**, thinly sliced
1 **garlic clove**, finely chopped
500 g (1 lb) **potatoes**, peeled
    and cut into 3.5 cm
    (1½ inch) chunks
100 g (3½ oz) shelled **fresh or**
    frozen peas
handful of **flat leaf parsley**,
    roughly chopped
salt and **pepper**

Trim the stalks of the artichokes, leaving about 3 cm (1¼ inches). Pull off and discard the tough outer leaves, exposing the paler tender leaves, then cut off their tips. Using a potato peeler, peel the stalk and dark green base until you see the lighter, yellowy flesh. Halve the artichokes and scoop out the hairy choke with a teaspoon and discard. Put in a bowl of cold water with the lemon juice to prevent discolouring.

Heat the oil in a large, heavy-based saucepan with a tight-fitting lid just large enough to hold the artichokes and potatoes in a single layer. Add the shallots and cook over a medium heat for 8–10 minutes until softened and translucent. Add the garlic and cook, stirring, for 1 minute. Toss in the drained artichokes, potatoes and salt and pepper.

Pour in enough water to come a quarter of the way up the vegetables. Bring to the boil, then reduce to a slow simmer. Cover with greaseproof paper and the lid. Cook for 45 minutes. Stir in the peas and parsley and cook for a further 5 minutes, or until the artichokes and potatoes are tender.

For braised courgettes, peas & prosciutto, omit the artichokes and potatoes. Cut 75 g (3 oz) prosciutto into thin strips and cook with the shallots as above. Once the garlic has cooked for 1 minute, stir in 2 courgettes, cut into 1 cm (½ inch) slices. Complete the recipe as above, but using 2 tablespoons chopped mint instead of the parsley.

sicilian caponata

Serves **4**

Preparation time **15 minutes**, plus standing

Cooking time **30 minutes**

100 ml (3½ fl oz) **olive oil**

2 **aubergines**, cut into 3.5 cm (1½ inch) cubes

1 large **onion**, coarsely chopped

3 **celery sticks**, sliced

50 g (2 oz) **pine nuts**

2 **garlic cloves**, chopped

400 g (13 oz) can **plum tomatoes**, drained and roughly chopped

2 tablespoons **capers in brine**, rinsed

50 g (2 oz) **pitted green olives**

3 tablespoons **red wine vinegar**

1 tablespoon **caster sugar**

6 **basil leaves**

salt and **pepper**

Heat the oil in a large frying pan over a high heat until the oil begins to shimmer. Add the aubergines, in batches, and cook, stirring frequently, for 5–6 minutes until they are golden and tender. Use a slotted spoon to transfer to a bowl.

Pour away all but 2 tablespoons oil from the pan. Add the onion, celery and pine nuts and cook over a low heat for 10 minutes until the vegetables are softened and lightly golden. Return the aubergines to the pan and stir in the remaining ingredients, except for the basil. Season with salt and pepper.

Bring the pan to the boil, then reduce the heat and simmer for 5 minutes. Stir in the basil. Remove from the heat and leave to stand for at least 15 minutes to allow the flavours to mingle. Serve warm or cold, as an antipasto, side dish or as a vegetarian main course, with some bread on the side.

For potato & pepper caponata, peel and cut 500 g (1 lb) potatoes into 3.5 cm (1½ inch) cubes. Cook in a saucepan of salted boiling water until tender, then drain. Omit the aubergine. Reduce the oil to 4 tablespoons and heat in a frying pan. Add the onion, celery and pine nuts with 2 red peppers, cored, deseeded and cut into large chunks, and cook as above. Toss in the potatoes and the remaining ingredients as above, but using black olives in place of the green. Season with salt and pepper, then follow the final step above to complete.

peperonata

Serves **4**
Preparation time **10 minutes**,
 plus preparing the peppers
Cooking time **45 minutes**

2 large **red peppers**, grilled,
 skinned, cored and
 deseeded (see page 28)
2 large **yellow peppers**,
 grilled, skinned, cored and
 deseeded (see page 28)
2 teaspoons **olive oil**
1 small **onion**, finely chopped
2 **garlic cloves**, finely chopped
400 g (13 oz) can **plum
 tomatoes**, roughly chopped
6 large **basil leaves**, torn
extra virgin olive oil, for
 drizzling (optional)
salt

Cut the peppers into wide strips and set aside.

Heat the oil in a heavy-based saucepan over a low
heat. Add the onion and cook, stirring occasionally,
for 10 minutes. Add the garlic and cook, stirring, for
1 minute. Add the tomatoes and their juice and the
pepper strips. Season with salt and bring to the boil.
Reduce the heat to a gentle simmer and cook, stirring
occasionally, for 25 minutes.

Stir the basil into the pan and cook for a further
5–10 minutes until the sauce has reduced. Drizzle
with extra virgin olive oil before serving, if liked. Serve
immediately as a side dish, or spoon over soft polenta or
stir into pasta. Alternatively, serve cold as an antipasto.

For caper & lemon peperonata, follow the recipe as
above also adding 2 tablespoons capers and the
grated zest of 1 lemon to the pan with the basil.

spinach & pea frittata

Serves **4**

Preparation time **10 minutes**

Cooking time **25 minutes**

1 tablespoon **olive oil**

1 **onion**, thinly sliced

150 g (5 oz) **baby spinach**

125 g (4 oz) shelled **fresh** or **frozen peas**

6 **eggs**

salt and **pepper**

Heat the oil in a heavy-based, ovenproof, nonstick 23 cm (9 inch) frying pan over a low heat. Add the onion and cook for 6–8 minutes until softened, then stir in the spinach and peas and cook for a further 2 minutes, or until any moisture released by the spinach has evaporated.

Beat the eggs in a bowl and season lightly with salt and pepper. Stir in the cooked vegetables, then pour the mixture into the pan and quickly arrange the vegetables so that they are evenly dispersed. Cook over a low heat for 8–10 minutes, or until all but the top of the frittata is set.

Transfer the pan to a preheated very hot grill and cook about 10 cm (4 inches) from the heat source until the top is set but not coloured. Give the pan a shake to loosen the frittata, then transfer to a plate to cool. Serve slightly warm or at room temperature, accompanied by a green salad.

For courgette, pea & cheese frittata, follow the first step above, but replace the spinach with 1 large courgette, coarsely grated. Add 4 tablespoons freshly grated Parmesan cheese and 100 g (3½ oz) cubed mozzarella cheese to the raw egg mixture with the vegetables and cook as above.

braised black cabbage & borlotti

Serves **4**

Preparation time **10 minutes**

Cooking time **30 minutes**

1.5 kg (3 lb) **cavolo nero (black cabbage)**

3 tablespoons **olive oil**

2 **garlic cloves**, thinly sliced

¼ teaspoon **crushed dried chillies**

400 g (13 oz) can **borlotti beans**, drained and rinsed

salt

Remove the thick stalks of the cabbage by holding the stems with one hand and using the other hand to strip away the leaves. Discard the stalks. Cook the leaves in a saucepan of boiling water for 15 minutes until just tender, then drain thoroughly.

Heat the oil in a large frying pan over a low heat. Add the garlic, crushed chillies and borlotti beans and cook for 5 minutes, then stir in the cooked cabbage. Season with salt and cook, stirring, for 6–8 minutes until the cabbage has completely wilted and absorbed the flavours. Serve immediately.

For spinach with pine nuts, follow the recipe above from the second step onwards, replacing the borlotti beans with 50 g (2 oz) pine nuts. Use 500 g (1 lb) baby spinach, instead of the cabbage, toss into the pan raw and cook, stirring, for 2–3 minutes until wilted. Stir a light grating of nutmeg into the cooked spinach before serving.

potato & green bean bake

Serves **4**
Preparation time **10 minutes**
Cooking time **45 minutes**

500 g (1 lb) **floury potatoes**,
peeled and cut into
large chunks
300 g (10 oz) **green beans**,
trimmed and halved
2 **garlic cloves**, finely chopped
handful of **basil leaves**, torn
100 g (3½ oz) **Parmesan
cheese**, freshly grated
200 g (7 oz) **ricotta cheese**
3 **eggs**, lightly beaten
100 g (3½ oz) **fresh white
breadcrumbs**
2 tablespoons **olive oil**, plus
extra for oiling
salt and **pepper**

Simmer the potatoes in a saucepan of salted boiling water for 10 minutes, then add the beans and cook for a further 3–4 minutes until the potatoes are cooked through and the beans are just tender. Drain, return to the pan and mash to a lumpy purée.

Stir the garlic, basil, cheeses and eggs into the vegetable purée and season with salt and pepper.

Sprinkle an oiled cake tin or ovenproof dish with a thin layer of the breadcrumbs. Pile in the vegetable mash, sprinkle with the remaining breadcrumbs and drizzle with the oil. Bake in a preheated oven, 200°C (400°F), Gas Mark 6, for 25–30 minutes until the topping is crisp and golden.

For potato, olive & sunblush tomato bake, cook the potatoes and mash as above, but omit the beans. Stir the garlic, eggs and cheeses into the mash as above together with 50 g (2 oz) roughly chopped pitted black olives and 8 roughly chopped sunblush tomatoes, replacing the basil with ½ teaspoon dried oregano. Follow the final step above to complete.

lemon panna cotta & raspberries

Serves **6**

Preparation time **10 minutes**, plus chilling and marinating

Cooking time **5 minutes**

600 ml (1 pint) **double cream**

100 g (3½ oz) **caster sugar**

pared **rind** of 2 **lemons**

1 **vanilla pod**, split lengthways and seeds removed

350 ml (12 fl oz) **milk**

3 teaspoons **powdered gelatine**

100 g (3½ oz) **fresh raspberries**

5 **mint leaves**, roughly chopped

3 tablespoons **grappa**

Put the cream, sugar, lemon rind and vanilla seeds in a saucepan. Bring to the boil over a low heat, then remove from the heat and leave to infuse for 5 minutes.

Meanwhile, bring the milk to the boil in a separate saucepan. Remove from the heat and carefully sprinkle with the gelatine, in as thin and even a layer as you can manage. Leave to stand for 2–3 minutes until the gelatine no longer looks dry, then stir to dissolve.

Strain the infused cream through a sieve into the milk and pour the mixture into 6 x 175 ml (6 fl oz) dariole moulds. Cover each with clingfilm and chill for at least 5 hours until set. It will keep for up to 3 days in the refrigerator.

Combine the raspberries, mint and grappa in a bowl. Cover and leave to marinate at room temperature for 30 minutes and up to 4 hours.

Unmould the panna cotta by carefully dipping the base and sides of the moulds in warm water for a few seconds. Invert on to individual serving plates and serve with the marinated raspberries.

For coffee-cream liqueur panna cotta, omit the lemon rind and the first step above. Dissolve the gelatine in the milk, as in the second step, then stir in 300 ml (½ pint) each coffee-flavoured cream liqueur and double cream. Pour into the dariole moulds and chill as above. Instead of the marinated raspberries, serve with the coffee sauce on page 142.

lemon & ricotta tart

Serves **8–10**

Preparation time **15 minutes**, plus chilling

Cooking time **50–55 minutes**

350 g (11½ oz) **ready-made sweet shortcrust pastry**
plain flour, for dusting
4 **eggs**
100 g (3½ oz) **caster sugar**
350 g (11½ oz) **ricotta cheese**
400 ml (14 fl oz) **double cream**
rind and **juice** of 3 **lemons**
fresh berries, to decorate

Roll the pastry out on a lightly floured work surface. Use to line a 23 cm (9 inch) fluted tart tin, then chill for 10 minutes. Line the pastry case with greaseproof paper and fill with baking beans.

Bake the pastry case in a preheated oven, 180°C (350°F), Gas Mark 4, for 10 minutes. Remove the baking beans and paper and bake for a further 5 minutes until golden.

Whisk the remaining ingredients together in a bowl and use to fill the pastry case. Reduce the oven temperature to 150°C (300°F), Gas Mark 2, and bake the tart for 35–40 minutes until just set. Serve with fresh berries, such as strawberries and blueberries, and a generous dusting of icing sugar.

For chocolate & ricotta tart, make and bake the pastry case as above. Then make the filling as above, but omit the lemon rind and juice and increase the double cream to 500 ml (17 fl oz). Stir in 100 g (3½ oz) roughly chopped plain dark chocolate. Use to fill the pastry case and bake as above.

pear & almond cake

Serves **8**
Preparation time **20 minutes**
Cooking time **35 minutes**

125 g (4 oz) **unsalted butter**,
  softened, plus extra for
  greasing
125 g (4 oz) **caster sugar**
2 large **eggs**, beaten
50 g (2 oz) **plain flour**, sifted
100 g (3½ oz) **ground
  almonds**
½ teaspoon **baking powder**
3 **ripe pears**, peeled, halved
  and cored
50 g (2 oz) **flaked almonds**
icing sugar, for dusting

Beat the butter and caster sugar together in a bowl until pale and fluffy. Add the eggs, a little at a time, beating well after each addition. If the mixture starts to curdle, add 1 tablespoon of the flour. Fold in the flour, ground almonds and baking powder using a large metal spoon and tip into a greased 20 cm (8 inch) spring form cake tin and use a palette knife to even out the mixture.

Arrange the pear halves over the top of the cake and bake in a preheated oven, 190°C (375°F), Gas Mark 5, for 25 minutes. Sprinkle the flaked almonds over the top and return to the oven for a further 10 minutes. The cake is ready when a skewer inserted into the centre of the cake comes out clean.

Leave the cake to cool in the tin, then carefully remove the ring and base. Dust with icing sugar before serving with Mascarpone, Marsala & Orange Cream (see below), if liked.

For mascarpone, Marsala & orange cream, to serve as an accompaniment, whisk the grated rind of 1 orange and 2 tablespoons of its juice in a bowl with 2 tablespoons sweet Marsala and 100 g (3½ oz) mascarpone cheese. Sweeten with icing sugar to taste.

caramel panna cotta & apricots

Serves **4**

Preparation time **30 minutes**, plus standing, cooling and chilling

Cooking time **15 minutes**

600 ml (1 pint) **double cream**
125 g (4 oz) **caster sugar**
1 **vanilla pod**, split lengthways
75 ml (3 fl oz) **granulated sugar**
2 tablespoons **water**
4 tablespoons **milk**
1 tablespoon **powdered gelatine**

Apricots

8 **ripe apricots**, halved, stoned and cut into thirds
150 ml (¼ pint) **water**
75 g (3 oz) **caster sugar**
1 **vanilla pod**, split lengthways

Put the cream, caster sugar and vanilla pod in a saucepan and heat until just below boiling point, stirring occasionally. Remove from the heat and leave to infuse for 20 minutes.

Meanwhile, heat the granulated sugar in the measurement water in a heavy-based saucepan until it has dissolved, then boil until the syrup turns to a golden caramel. Quickly pour into 4 x 150 ml (¼ pint) ramekins or small moulds. Set on a tray and leave to harden.

Pour the milk into a small saucepan and sprinkle on the gelatine. Warm over a low heat until the gelatine dissolves. Stir into the infused cream mixture. Bring to the boil, then immediately remove from the heat and strain through a sieve into a jug. Pour into the ramekins or moulds. Leave to cool, then for at least 5 hours, until set.

Put the apricots in a small saucepan with the measurement water, sugar and vanilla pod. Bring slowly to the boil, then cover and simmer gently for 5–8 minutes until just tender. Leave to cool, then remove the vanilla pod, cover and chill.

Carefully loosen the panna cottas and turn out on to individual serving plates. Serve with the apricots.

For citrus peel panna cotta, scatter 50 g (2 oz) chopped citrus peel over the set caramel, before filling the ramekins or moulds with the panna cotta mixture. Omit the apricot sauce and serve instead with a drizzle of Limoncello liqueur.

zabaglione semifreddo with coffee

Serves **6**
Preparation time **15 minutes**, plus freezing
Cooking time **10 minutes**

6 **egg yolks**
100 g (3½ oz) **caster sugar**
100 ml (3½ fl oz) **sweet Marsala**
300 ml (½ pint) **double cream**
30 **sponge fingers**

Coffee sauce
200 ml (7 fl oz) **cold espresso coffee**
100 g (3½ oz) **granulated sugar**
3 tablespoons **coffee-flavoured liqueur**

Whisk the egg yolks with the caster sugar in a heatproof bowl set over a saucepan of gently simmering water until the sugar has melted. Add the Marsala and continue whisking for another 6–8 minutes, or until the mixture has thickened and holds its shape.

Whip the cream in a bowl until soft peaks form. Gently fold in the egg mixture. Roughly break the sponge fingers, then fold into the zabaglione. Tip into a 1 kg (2 lb) loaf tin lined with clingfilm. Cover with clingfilm and freeze for at least 6 hours or overnight until set.

Make the coffee sauce. Heat the coffee in a small saucepan, add the granulated sugar and stir until melted. Add the liqueur and boil vigorously until the sauce becomes thick and syrupy.

Turn the semifreddo out on to a serving plate and spoon over the sauce, which can be warm or at room temperature. Serve cut into slices.

For individual zabaglione semifreddos with raspberry sauce, make the zabaglione mixture as above and set in 6 dariole moulds lined with clingfilm. In place of the coffee sauce, heat 150 g (5 oz) raspberries in a small saucepan with 1 tablespoon caster sugar and 50 ml (2 fl oz) apple juice. Bring to the boil, then simmer gently for 2 minutes. Crush the berries with the back of a fork and squeeze in the juice of ½ lemon. Invert the semifreddos on to individual plates and serve with the sauce.

chocolate sorbet

Makes about **900 ml**
  (1½ pints)
Preparation time **15 minutes**,
  plus chilling and freezing
Cooking time **10 minutes**

600 ml (1 pint) **water**
150 g (5 oz) **soft dark brown
  sugar**
200 g (7 oz) **granulated
  sugar**
65 g (2½ oz) **unsweetened
  cocoa powder**
25 g (1 oz) **plain dark
  chocolate with 70% cocoa
  solids**, finely chopped
2½ teaspoons **vanilla extract**
1 teaspoon **instant espresso
  coffee powder**

Put the measurement water, sugars and cocoa powder in a saucepan and mix together. Heat gently, stirring until the sugar has dissolved. Increase the heat to bring the mixture to a boil, then reduce to a simmer for 8 minutes.

Remove the pan from the heat and stir in the chocolate, vanilla extract and espresso powder until thoroughly dissolved. Pour into a bowl and cool over ice or leave to cool and chill.

Freeze in an ice-cream machine according to the manufacturer's instructions. Serve immediately or transfer to a chilled plastic freezerproof container and store in the freezer for up to 1 month. If you are using the sorbet straight from the freezer, transfer to the refrigerator 20 minutes before serving to soften slightly.

For rum & chocolate-chip sorbet, replace the vanilla extract with 3 tablespoons dark rum. Stir 75 g (3 oz) chopped plain dark chocolate into the ice-cream mixture before churning.

classic tiramisu

Serves **4**

Preparation time **20 minutes**,
plus chilling

3 **eggs**, separated
125 g (4 oz) **caster sugar**
250 g (8 oz) **mascarpone
cheese**
200 ml (7 fl oz) **cold espresso
coffee**
4 tablespoons **sweet Marsala**
32–34 **sponge fingers**
75 g (3 oz) **plain dark
chocolate**, grated

Whisk the egg yolks and sugar in a bowl with a hand-
held electric whisk until light, airy and the beaters leave
a trail when lifted. Put the mascarpone in a large bowl
and beat in one-third of the egg mixture until smooth,
then fold in the remaining egg mixture. Beat the egg
whites in a separate bowl until they hold their shape
and have a consistency resembling shaving foam. Fold
into the mascarpone mixture.

Pour the coffee and Marsala into a shallow bowl and
dip in the sponge fingers until soaked on both sides
but not all the way through. Arrange a layer of tightly
packed biscuits in four 10 cm (4 inch) bowls. Spread
with half the mascarpone mixture, then top with a
second layer of soaked sponge fingers. Use the
remaining mascarpone mixture to cover the sponge
fingers. Cover with clingfilm and chill for at least 3 hours
or up to overnight.

Just before serving, remove the tiramisu from the
refrigerator and dust with the grated chocolate.

For blackberry & lemon tiramisu, make the
mascarpone mixture as above, but add 125 g (4 oz)
crushed blackberries and the finely grated rind of
1 lemon at the end of the first step. Complete the
recipe as above, but decorate the top with
blackberries before dusting with grated chocolate.

hazelnut chocolate ice cream

Serves **4**
Preparation time **10 minutes**,
   plus freezing
Cooking time **5 minutes**

150 g (5 oz) **blanched
   hazelnuts**
350 g (11½ oz) **hazelnut and
   chocolate spread**
400 g (13 oz) can **evaporated
   milk**

Roughly crush the hazelnuts, then toast in a frying pan over a low heat until lightly golden. Leave to cool.

Tip the spread into a bowl and stir in a quarter of the evaporated milk until you have a smooth mixture. Stir in the remaining evaporated milk, then fold in 100 g (3½ oz) toasted hazelnuts.

Churn in an ice-cream machine according to the manufacturer's instructions. Transfer to a plastic freezerproof container and freeze.

Alternatively, freeze the mixture in a shallow container or tray for 2 hours until half-frozen, then tip into a bowl and whisk thoroughly to break up any ice crystals that may have formed. Return the mixture to the container and the freezer. Repeat the process at hourly intervals until the mixture is smooth and almost set. Finally, transfer the ice cream to a plastic freezerproof container and freeze until firm.

Remove the ice cream from the freezer 10 minutes before serving to soften slightly; it is best eaten within 48 hours. Scatter with the remaining hazelnuts and serve.

For speedy chunky chocolate ice cream, tip a 400 g (13 oz) tub good-quality chocolate ice cream into a bowl and leave to soften slightly. Lightly crush 75 g (3 oz) chocolate wafer biscuits and vigorously stir into the ice cream. Transfer to a plastic freezerproof container and freeze. Remove from the freezer and leave to soften slightly as above before serving.

sweet pastry ribbons

Makes about **35 ribbons**
Preparation time **25 minutes**
Cooking time **10 minutes**

1 **egg**
pinch of **salt**
2 tablespoons **vin santo** or
  sweet Marsala
4 drops of **vanilla extract**
1½ tablespoons **caster sugar**
175 g (6 oz) **plain flour**, plus
  extra for dusting
sunflower oil, for deep-frying
icing sugar, for dusting

Put the egg, salt, vin santo or Marsala, vanilla extract and caster sugar in a food processor and pulse until combined. Add the flour and pulse again until you have a firm dough. Knead on a work surface for 2 minutes until smooth and elastic.

Set a pasta machine at the largest opening. Cut the dough into 3 rectangular pieces. Run 1 rectangle through the machine. Fold in half widthways and run through again. Lower the setting by 1 notch and run the dough through again, then run once through each of the remaining settings. If the sheet becomes too long to handle, cut in half and run 1 half through at a time. If it becomes too sticky, dust with a little flour.

Lay the sheet on a surface dusted with flour and cover with a clean tea towel while you roll out the remaining dough. Use a sharp knife to cut the dough sheets into 3.5 cm (1½ inch) lengths.

Heat enough oil for deep-frying in a deep saucepan to 180–190°C (350–375°F), or until a cube of bread browns in 30 seconds. Add the ribbons, in batches, and cook for 30 seconds until golden all over. Drain on kitchen paper. Leave to cool completely, then generously dust with icing sugar. The ribbons can be stored in an airtight container for up to 2 days.

For honey & cinnamon pastry ribbons, replace the caster sugar with 1 tablespoon honey and use 1 teaspoon ground cinnamon instead of the vanilla extract. Prepare and cook as above.

watermelon & choc-chip sorbet

Serves **4–6**
Preparation time **20 minutes**,
   plus chilling and freezing
Cooking time **5 minutes**

750 g (1½ lb) **peeled**
   watermelon, deseeded
   and cubed
300 g (10 oz) **caster sugar**
8 tablespoons **lemon juice**
pink food colouring (optional)
1 **egg white**
125 g (4 oz) **chocolate chips**

Purée the watermelon in a food processor or blender. Add the sugar and process for 30 seconds.

Pour into a saucepan and bring slowly to the boil, stirring until the sugar has dissolved, then simmer for 1 minute. Remove from the heat, add the lemon juice, then leave to cool, adding a few drops of pink food colouring, if liked. Chill for at least 1 hour or overnight.

Use an ice-cream machine for the best results. Half-freeze the mixture according to the manufacturer's instructions, then lightly whisk the egg white and add with the motor running still running. Stir in the chocolate chips, then transfer to a plastic freezerproof container and freeze until firm.

Alternatively, freeze the mixture in a shallow freezer tray until frozen around the edges, then mash well with a fork. Whisk the egg white until stiff in a bowl. Drop spoonfuls of the sorbet into the egg white while whisking constantly with a hand-held electric whisk until the mixture is thick and foamy. Return to the freezer to firm up, then stir in the chocolate chips when almost frozen. Freeze until firm.

Transfer the sorbet to the refrigerator for 20 minutes before serving to soften. Serve with dessert biscuits.

For watermelon & orange sorbet, omit the cinnamon and chocolate chips. Reduce the quantity of watermelon to 500 g (1 lb) and process to a purée. Heat the sugar in a pan with 250 ml (8 fl oz) freshly squeezed orange juice, stirring until dissolved. Once cooled combine the watermelon, sweetened orange juice and lemon juice. Freeze as above.

frozen bellini

Serves **4**
Preparation time **15 minutes**

750 g (1½ lb) **ripe peaches**,
   stoned
100 ml (3½ fl oz) **sweet
   sparkling wine**
juice of ½ **lemon**
1 tablespoon **icing sugar**, plus
   extra to taste
15 **ice cubes**

Put 500 g (1 lb) of the peaches in a blender and blend
to a purée. Transfer to a large bowl. Slice the remaining
fruit, put in a separate bowl and gently toss with the wine.

Whizz the lemon juice, icing sugar and ice cubes in the
blender until the ice is well crushed – you may need to
do this in stages to avoid overheating the blender.

Transfer the crushed ice mixture to the bowl with the
fruit and stir well to combine thoroughly. Taste, adding
more icing sugar if necessary, and serve immediately,
topped with the sliced fruit.

For cheat's strawberry & balsamic granita, replace
the peaches with 625 g (1¼ lb) strawberries, hulled.
Purée 500 g (1 lb) of the strawberries, then quarter the
remaining strawberries and stir into 2 tablespoons
aged balsamic vinegar, instead of the sparkling wine.
Complete the recipe as above.

pistachio & pine nut biscotti

Makes **50**
Preparation time **20 minutes**,
 plus cooling
Cooking time **50 minutes–
 1 hour**

175 g (6 oz) **shelled pistachio
 nuts**
2 tablespoons **pine nuts**
125 g (4 oz) **unsalted butter**,
 softened, plus extra for
 greasing
200 g (7 oz) **granulated
 sugar**
2 **eggs**, beaten
finely grated **rind** of 1 **lemon**
1 tablespoon **Amaretto di
 Saronno**
about 375 g (12 oz) **plain
 flour**, plus extra for dusting
1½ teaspoons **baking powder**
½ teaspoon **salt**
75 g (3 oz) **coarse polenta**

Spread the pistachios and pine nuts out on a baking
sheet and toast in a preheated oven, 160°C (325°F),
Gas Mark 3, for 5–10 minutes until golden. Remove
the nuts and leave to cool but leave the oven on.

Beat the butter and sugar together in a large bowl
until just mixed, then beat in the eggs, lemon rind
and Amaretto. Sift the flour, baking powder and salt
together into a separate bowl, then stir into the butter
mixture with the polenta. Stir in the toasted pistachios
and pine nuts.

Turn the dough out on to a floured work surface and
knead until smooth, working in a little more flour if too
sticky. Divide into quarters and roll each quarter into a
sausage 5 cm (2 inches) long and 1.5 cm (¾ inch)
thick. Flatten slightly. Place on 2 greased baking sheets
and bake in the oven for about 35 minutes until just
golden around the edges.

Leave to cool slightly, then cut on the diagonal into
1 cm (½ inch) thick slices. Place, cut-side down, on the
baking sheets and bake for a further 10–15 minutes
until golden brown and crisp, being careful not to burn.
Transfer to a wire rack to cool.

For almond & chocolate biscotti, replace the
pistachios and pine nuts with 200 g (7 oz) blanched
almonds and toast them as above. When adding
the almonds to the biscuit dough also include
100 g (3½ oz) roughly chopped plain chocolate.
Shape and bake as above.

index

almond & chocolate biscotti 156
anchovies *see* seafood
apricots: caramel panna cotta & apricots 140
artichokes: braised artichokes & potatoes 122
  prosciutto & artichoke sfincione 52
asparagus: & pancetta risotto 74
  asparagus, pea & mint risotto 74
  cheesy prosciutto-wrapped asparagus 22
  pasta salad with mozzarella & asparagus 48
  spaghetti with charred asparagus 48
aubergine: & courgette parmigiana 120
  aubergine, basil & ricotta pizza 56

balsamic figs with parma ham 16
barley, bean & porcini soup 58
basil & lemon batter 8
batter: basil & lemon 8
beans: barley, bean & porcini soup 58
  borlotti, pasta & red mullet soup 58
  braised black cabbage & borlotti 130
  broad bean bruschetta 12
  mixed bean salad 26
  parmesan & cannellini bean bruschetta 12
  potato & green bean bake 132
  tuna & borlotti bean salad 26
  white bean soup 64
beef: classic meatloaf 98
  devilled fillet steaks 108
  steak sandwich with red pesto 106
  see also liver; meatballs
bellini, frozen 154
biscotti: almond & chocolate 156
  pistachio & pine nut 156

black cabbage: braised black cabbage & borlotti 130
blackberry & lemon tiramisu 146
borlotti *see* beans
bread: roasted tomato, bread & balsamic soup 66
  tomato & bread soup 66
  see also bruschetta; grissini
broccoli: orecchiette with 34
bruschetta: broad bean 12
  parmesan & cannellini bean 12

cake: pear & almond 138
caper & lemon peperonata 126
caponata: potato & pepper 124
  sicilian 124
caramel panna cotta & apricots 140
carpaccio: fresh swordfish 14
  fresh tuna 14
cauliflower: penne with creamy cauliflower 34
cheese: aubergine, basil & ricotta pizza 56
  baked polenta with gorgonzola 78
  cheesy polenta & mushrooms 82
  cheesy polenta with mushrooms & tomato 82
  cheesy prosciutto-wrapped asparagus 22
  chocolate & ricotta tart 136
  courgette & smoked mozzarella pizza 56
  courgette, pea & cheese frittata 128
  griddled courgettes with lemon, mint & parmesan 24
  lemon & ricotta tart 136
  mozzarella in carrozza 20
  mushroom, blue cheese & spinach lasagne 36
  parmesan & cannellini bean bruschetta 12
  pasta salad with mozzarella & asparagus 48
  pizza with smoked mozzarella, parma ham & rocket 54
  pizza with speck & dolcelatte 54

spiced parma ham & mozzarella in carrozza 20
chestnut, rice & pancetta soup 60
chicken: chicken liver & caramelized onions 100
  devilled breasts 108
  milanese 116
  roast chicken with herbs & garlic 118
  roast chicken with lemon & sage 118
  with olives & rosemary 110
chilli: spaghetti with clams & chilli 38
  toasted garlic & chilli oil 64
chocolate: & ricotta tart 136
  almond & chocolate biscotti 156
  hazelnut chocolate ice cream 148
  rum & chocolate-chip sorbet 144
  sorbet 144
  speedy chunky chocolate ice cream 148
  watermelon & choc-chip sorbet 152
  citrus peel panna cotta 140
clams *see* seafood
cod *see* seafood
coffee: coffee-cream liqueur panna cotta 134
  zabaglione semifreddo with coffee 142
courgettes: & smoked mozzarella pizza 56
  aubergine & courgette parmigiana 120
  braised courgettes, peas & prosciutto 122
  courgette, pea & cheese frittata 128
  griddled with lemon, mint & parmesan 24
  prawn, courgette & saffron risotto 76
cream: mascarpone, marsala & orange 138
crudités & garlic anchovy dip 32

devilled chicken breasts 108
devilled fillet steaks 108
dips: crudités & garlic anchovy 32
  tomato & basil 80
dolcelatte *see* cheese

fennel: & olive parmigiana 120
  fennel, rice & pancetta soup with garlic & anchovies 60
  sardines stuffed with 90
  spaghetti with sardine & fennel sauce 90
fettuccine *see* pasta
figs: balsamic figs with parma ham 16
fish *see* seafood
frittata: courgette, pea & cheese 128
  spinach & pea 128

garlic: & caper mayonnaise 32
  crudités & garlic anchovy dip 32
  fennel, rice & pancetta soup with garlic & anchovies 60
  roast garlic-studded monkfish 86
  rocket & garlic crumbed mussels 10
  sole with lemon, parsley & garlic 88
  toasted garlic & chilli oil 64
gorgonzola *see* cheese
granita: cheat's strawberry & balsamic 154
grissini: prosciutto-wrapped 22
ham: balsamic figs with parma ham 16
  braised courgettes, peas & prosciutto 122
  cheesy prosciutto-wrapped asparagus 22
  minted melon with parma ham 16
  pizza with smoked mozzarella, parma ham & rocket 54
  pizza with speck & dolcelatte 54
  prosciutto & artichoke sfincione 52
  prosciutto-wrapped grissini 22
  spiced parma ham & mozzarella in carrozza 20
hazelnut chocolate ice cream 148
honey & cinnamon pastry ribbons 150

ice cream: hazelnut
    chocolate 148
    speedy chunky chocolate
    148

lamb: cutlets with red pesto
    106
    leg of lamb with lemon &
    rosemary 102
    roast with wine & juniper
    102
    shanks braised in milk 104
lasagne see pasta
lemon: & ricotta tart 136
    basil & lemon batter 8
    blackberry & lemon
    tiramisu 146
    caper & lemon peperonata
    126
    lemon panna cotta &
    raspberries 134
    lemon, rocket & basil
    linguine 44
    tortellini with lemon, pea &
    basil sauce 44
    watercress & lemon risotto
    70
lentils: cod & lentils in tomato
    sauce 114
    sausages & lentils in
    tomato sauce 114
liver: calves' liver &
    caramelized onions
    100
    chicken liver & caramelized
    onions 100

mackerel see seafood
mascarpone see cheese
mayonnaise: garlic & caper 32
meatballs: in red wine sauce
    98
    pork meatballs in a tomato
    & red pepper sauce 46
    with spaghetti 46
meatloaf 98
melon: minted with parma
    ham 16
    watermelon & choc-chip
    sorbet 152
    watermelon & orange
    sorbet 152
    minted melon with parma
    ham 16
monkfish see seafood
mozzarella see cheese
mushrooms: barley, bean &
    porcini soup 58

cheesy polenta &
    mushrooms 82
cheesy polenta with
    mushrooms & tomato 82
fettuccine & dried porcini
    sauce 42
fettuccine with creamy
    mushroom & tarragon
    sauce 42
mushroom, blue cheese &
    spinach lasagne 36
wild mushroom lasagne 36
mussels see seafood

oil: toasted garlic & chilli 64
olives: fennel & olive
    parmigiana 120
    potato, olive & sunblush
    tomato bake 132
    roasted monkfish with olive
    paste 86
    tomatoes stuffed with rice,
    capers, anchovies &
    olives 72
    tuna with onion & olives
    92
orange: watermelon & orange
    sorbet 152
orecchiette see pasta

pancetta: asparagus &
    pancetta risotto 74
    chestnut, rice & pancetta
    soup 60
    fennel, rice & pancetta
    soup with garlic &
    anchovies 60
    pancetta, potato & fregola
    soup 62
    radicchio risotto with
    pancetta 70
    roasted tomato & pancetta
    pasta 40
    roasted tomato, pancetta &
    spinach salad 40
    spaghetti with clams,
    pancetta & tomatoes 38
panna cotta: caramel panna
    cotta & apricots 140
    citrus peel 140
    coffee-cream liqueur 134
    lemon panna cotta &
    raspberries 134
parma ham see ham
parmesan see cheese
parmigiana: aubergine &
    courgette 120
    fennel & olive 120

pasta: borlotti, pasta & red
    mullet soup 58
fettuccine & dried porcini
    sauce 42
fettuccine with creamy
    mushroom & tarragon
    sauce 42
lemon, rocket & basil
    linguine 44
meatballs with spaghetti
    46
mushroom, blue cheese &
    spinach lasagne 36
orecchiette with broccoli
    34
pancetta, potato & fregola
    soup 62
pasta salad with mozzarella
    & asparagus 48
penne with creamy
    cauliflower 34
roasted tomato & pancetta
    pasta 40
seafood & fregola soup 62
spaghetti with charred
    asparagus 48
spaghetti with clams & chilli
    38
spaghetti with clams,
    pancetta & tomatoes 38
spaghetti with sardine &
    fennel sauce 90
tortellini with lemon, pea &
    basil sauce 44
wild mushroom lasagne 36
pastry ribbons: honey &
    cinnamon 150
    sweet 150
pâté: salt cod 18
pear & almond cake 138
peas: asparagus, pea & mint
    risotto 74
    braised courgettes, peas &
    prosciutto 122
    courgette, pea & cheese
    frittata 128
    spinach & pea frittata 128
    tortellini with lemon, pea &
    basil sauce 44
penne see pasta
peppers: caper & lemon
    peperonata 126
    grilled in herb oil 28
    peperonata 126
    pork meatballs in a tomato
    & red pepper sauce 46
    potato & pepper caponata
    124

stuffed peppers 28
pesto, red 106
pine nuts: pistachio & pine
    nut biscotti 156
    spinach with pine nuts 130
pistachio & pine nut biscotti
    156
pizzas: aubergine, basil &
    ricotta 56
    basic pizza dough 7
    courgette & smoked
    mozzarella 56
    fiorentina 50
    prosciutto & artichoke
    sfincione 52
    spinach, anchovy & caper
    50
    tomato, onion and anchovy
    sfincione 52
    with smoked mozzarella,
    parma ham & rocket 54
    with speck & dolcelatte 54
polenta: baked polenta with
    gorgonzola 78
    cheesy polenta &
    mushrooms 82
    cheesy polenta with
    mushrooms & tomato 82
    griddled herbed polenta 78
    polenta chips 80
pork: braised in milk 104
    meatballs in a tomato &
    red pepper sauce 46
    roast herbed pork belly 112
    sausage & apricot stuffed
    pork 112
potato: & green bean bake
    132
    & pepper caponata 124
    braised artichokes &
    potatoes 122
    pancetta, potato & fregola
    soup 62
    potato, olive & sunblush
    tomato bake 132
    smoked mackerel with
    potato & salsa verde
    salad, 84
prawns see seafood
prosciutto see ham

rabbit in white wine &
    rosemary 110
radicchio risotto with pancetta
    70
raspberries: individual
    zabaglione semifreddos
    with raspberry sauce 142

lemon panna cotta & raspberries 134
red mullet see seafood
ribollita 68
rice: asparagus & pancetta risotto 74
asparagus, pea & mint risotto 74
chestnut, rice & pancetta soup 60
fennel, rice & pancetta soup with garlic & anchovies 60
prawn, courgette & saffron risotto 76
saffron risotto 76
seafood rice salad 30
tomatoes stuffed with rice 72
tomatoes stuffed with rice, capers, anchovies & olives 72
watercress & lemon risotto 70
ricotta see cheese
risotto see rice
rocket: lemon, rocket & basil linguine 44
pizza with smoked mozzarella, parma ham & rocket 54
rocket & garlic crumbed mussels 10
rum & chocolate-chip sorbet 144

saffron: risotto 76
prawn, courgette & saffron risotto 76
salads: mixed bean 26
pasta salad with mozzarella & asparagus 48
roasted tomato, pancetta & spinach 40
seafood 30
seafood rice 30
tuna & borlotti bean 26
salsa verde 84

smoked mackerel with potato & salsa verde salad 84
sausage: & apricot stuffed pork 112
& lentils in tomato sauce 114
scallops see seafood
seafood: & fregola soup 62
borlotti, pasta & red mullet soup 58
carpaccio of fresh tuna 14
cod & lentils in tomato sauce 114
crudités & garlic anchovy dip 32
fennel, rice & pancetta soup with garlic & anchovies 60
fried calamari 96
mussels alla marinara 94
prawn, courgette & saffron risotto 76
red mullet with salsa verde 84
roast garlic-studded monkfish 86
roasted monkfish with olive paste 86
rocket & garlic crumbed mussels 10
salt cod in batter 18
salt cod pâté 18
sardines stuffed with fennel 90
seafood rice salad 30
seafood salad 30
smoked mackerel with potato & salsa verde salad, 84
sole with lemon, parsley & garlic 88
sole with tomatoes & capers 88
spaghetti with clams & chilli 38
spaghetti with clams, pancetta & tomatoes 38

spaghetti with sardine & fennel sauce 90
spicy fried prawns 96
spinach, anchovy & caper pizza 50
squid alla marinara 94
swordfish carpaccio 14
swordfish with onion & sultanas 92
tomato & parsley crumbed scallops 10
tomato, onion and anchovy sfincione 52
tomatoes stuffed with rice, capers, anchovies & olives 72
tuna & borlotti bean salad 26
tuna with onion & olives 92
sfincione see pizza
smoked mackerel see seafood
sole see seafood
sorbet: chocolate 144
rum & chocolate-chip 144
watermelon & choc-chip 152
watermelon & orange 152
spaghetti see pasta
speck see ham
spinach: & pea frittata 128
mushroom, blue cheese & spinach lasagne 36
pizza fiorentina 50
roasted tomato, pancetta & spinach salad 40
spinach, anchovy & caper pizza 50
with pine nuts 130
squid see seafood
steak see beef
strawberry: cheat's strawberry & balsamic granita 154
sweet pastry ribbons 150
swordfish see seafood

tarts: chocolate & ricotta 136
lemon & ricotta 136

tiramisu 146
blackberry & lemon 146
tomato: & basil dip 80
& bread soup 66
& parsley crumbed scallops 10
cheesy polenta with mushrooms & tomato 82
pork meatballs in a tomato & red pepper sauce 46
potato, olive & sunblush tomato bake 132
roasted tomato & pancetta pasta 40
roasted tomato, bread & balsamic soup 66
roasted tomato, pancetta & spinach salad 40
sausages & lentils in tomato sauce 114
sole with tomatoes & capers 88
spaghetti with clams, pancetta & tomatoes 38
stuffed with rice 72
stuffed with rice, capers, anchovies & olives 72
tomato, onion and anchovy sfincione 52
tortellini see pasta
tuna see seafood
turkey milanese 116

vegetables (mixed): fried vegetables in batter 8
griddled vegetable platter 24

watercress & lemon risotto 70
watermelon see melon
white bean soup 64
wild mushroom lasagne 36

zabaglione: semifreddo with coffee 142
semifreddos with raspberry sauce 142

acknowledgements

Executive Editor Nicky Hill
Editor Kerenza Swift
Executive Art Editor Geoff Fennel
Designer Joanna MacGregor
Photographer Stephen Conroy
Home Economist Marina Filippelli

Props Stylist Liz Hippisley
Production Controller Carolin Stransky
Commissioned Photography: © Octopus Publishing Group Ltd/Stephen Conroy. Other photography © Octopus Publishing Group Ltd.